BEFORE THE M
SAILING SH

BY

CAPTAIN JOHN MASON, R.N.R. (RETIRED)
EXTRA CERTIFICATED MASTER

Author of

THE YOUNG MATE'S DAILY COMPANION, OR PRACTICAL
SEAMANSHIP SIMPLIFIED

and

SHIPMASTERS AND THEIR DIFFICULTIES ABROAD

KIRKWALL :
W. R. MACKINTOSH, *The Orcadian* OFFICE
1928

Printing Statement:

Due to the very old age and scarcity of this book,
many of the pages may be hard to read due to the
blurring of the original text, possible missing pages,
missing text and other issues beyond our control.

Because this is such an important and rare work, we
believe it is best to reproduce this book regardless of
its original condition.

Thank you for your understanding.

PREFACE.

As I seldom read a preface, unless it be as an after-thought, it would now be inconsistent on my part to state more than is absolutely necessary.

In the ever-growing library of sailing-ship literature, I trust there is still room for an unpretentious book, written by one who has spent forty-five years of his life at sea, trading to all parts of the world; in the last twenty-nine years, prior to my retirement two years ago, I was in command of four sailing ships and eight steamers, ranging from an 1800-ton sailing ship to a passenger liner of 13,850 tons gross.

It is my earnest wish to preserve the memory of the sailing ships and the men who manned them in the early eighties. I have endeavoured to write the book as plainly as possible, in the plain every-day language of the sea, without any pretence to literary merit.

At the present time a large sailing ship is a rarity, and the few that are afloat are sailing under foreign flags and manned by foreign crews.

The beauty of the sailing ship under full sail was a thing to be admired as she slid through the water gracefully, with the white foam curling under her bows. The men who manned those ships in the early eighties were of the real bull-dog breed, and commanded the admiration of the whole world. The sea was a hard school, and no place for weaklings or misfits of any kind.

CONTENTS.

BEFORE THE MAST IN SAILING SHIPS.

INTRODUCTORY.

THIS narrative is written with the object of giving present-day seafarers and landsmen alike an account of the fine sailing ships of the last two decades of the last century, *viz.*, the eighties and nineties, and of the fine lot of men who manned them. They played a very important part in building up our overseas Dominions and in keeping the British flag flying in every seaport of the world.

With all due credit to the officers and men of the present-day Mercantile Marine, I may safely say that none of them would care to undergo the hardships and privations that the crews of large sailing ships had to endure forty years ago. Our officers and men of the present day have not had the hard training under canvas which develops bone, muscle and nerve, and cultivates self-reliance under the most trying conditions. Time and again I have noticed that if a young man started a seafaring career in one of those ships he could never stick at it if he had reached the age of 20 or over; and one could always take it that every sailing ship officer, seaman and apprentice started his seafaring career very early in life, say from 14 to 18 years of age.

The seamen of the Mercantile Marine deserve no end of gratitude from their country for the services they rendered during the Great War. It is estimated that about 16,000 officers and men of the Mercantile Marine gave their lives for their country in the Great War. Enemy submarines, mines, shot and shell had no terrors for them. When other classes of men on shore tried to

B

hold the country to ransom, the men of the Mercantile Marine manned the ships without a murmur. Had it not been for them, this nation and her allies would have been starved into submission during the third year of the war.

The Royal Naval Reserve gave a good account of itself, as for instance, in the fight between the Cap Trafalgar and the Carmania. The Cap Trafalgar was a new German merchant vessel and the Carmania was a Cunard Line steamer. Both vessels were about the same size, and the Carmania in a very short time sent the Cap Trafalgar to the bottom, off the Brazilian coast. The Carmania had about 350 shot-holes pierced in her sides. Both ships were manned by merchant seamen, and the fight is considered to have been one of the best during the war.

Merchant ships during the first years of the war were terribly handicapped, as they were sent to sea without armament of any kind to protect them from the German submarines, and when they were eventually supplied with guns they were too small to compete with those of the enemy under-water craft.

So much for the seamen during the Great War.

Landsmen and even seamen of the present day can have only a hazy idea of what life was on the stately vessels of forty or fifty years ago, on some of which the writer spent three years before the mast. To their crews no land was too distant, no seas too difficult to navigate, no pestilential port too bad to visit, and no cargo too dangerous to carry. The food in many ships was scarcely fit to keep life in—being both scanty and bad at the same time. The forecastles were generally under the forecastle head and were flooded out when the hawse plugs were out. Many of the captains were hard men; but to give them their due, nearly all were splendid seamen, and the man who was not a driver and did not make good passages had to get out very soon to make room for a man who could.

The Brazilian ports simply reeked with yellow fever for eight months of the year, and during the interval smallpox raged. In Rio de Janeiro in 1894-1895 hundreds of men died from yellow fever; whole ship's crews were wiped out of existence in Rio and Santos.

In the beginning of 1896 an Italian man-of-war was reported to have lost nearly 300 men in Rio de Janeiro. The bodies of those who died of smallpox in the isolation hospital on Santa Barbara Island were taken to some place further up the harbour and thrown into quick-lime pits. When a man took smallpox on board a ship, the ensign had to be hoisted on the foremast as a signal for the port doctor. This official started on his round among the ships at nine in the morning in a steam launch. The sick man had to be brought down into the launch for examination, and the doctor would state where the man was to be taken. If the man had to be sent to hospital the ship's crew had to take him there.

In 1883 freights became so low that ships had to sail with smaller crews in order to make ends meet. Through this under-manning, hard work, and starvation, sailormen as a rule became so disgruntled at everything in connection with the ship that they deserted at nearly every port of any consequence that they went to, especially at Colonial and American ports. Even in Rio de Janeiro I have seen men desert their ships.

A ship would leave England for an Australian port, and on arrival sometimes the whole crew would desert. After a few days on shore they would ship in a vessel, say, bound for San Francisco. They would get a month's advance to clear them out of the boarding house, and to buy a suit of oilskins. On arrival at San Francisco they would desert again, and after a day or two on shore would be packed off in another ship bound for Europe—generally the Channel for orders, with three months' advance this time and nothing less. Not a penny of this advance went to them. When brought ashore they got a few drinks and were never allowed to be sober again until at sea. Ships, on an average, took four months from San Francisco to an English port, consequently the sailorman was very lucky if he arrived with a couple of pounds in his possession after probably a twelve months' cruise.

A HARD SHIP.

IN the early eighties the sailing ships had reached the zenith of their glory; the days of the wooden ships had passed. In every large seaport a dozen or more of them could be seen. It was in one of these large sailing vessels that I shipped in 1884 as able seaman on a voyage from Newcastle, New South Wales, to San Francisco, *via* Fort San Diego, with a cargo of coal. This was a Clyde-owned and Clyde-built vessel, a full-rigged ship of about 3200 tons burden and about three years old. As soon as I saw her lying at the buoys I was so greatly impressed with her fine lines, and her yards trimmed to a nicety, that I made up my mind to try and get away in her, as I understood that she wanted a full complement of able seamen at four pounds per month.

After signing on we were allowed two days' grace so as to give the men a chance to get over their spree before going on board. The boarding-house keepers got practically all the advance money from the men to pay for their keep and for a small outfit such as a cheap dongaree suit, and a " donkey's breakfast " (straw bed). As there was a large demand in San Francisco at that time for Newcastle coal, the seamen required to man the ships necessary for its transport were rather scarce.

On the day on which we were ordered on board, we had to take boat from the Market Wharf to convey us and our belongings to the ship where she lay in the stream. Three of us were from the Sailors' Home and the other thirteen from sailors' boarding houses, all of whom were more or less under the influence of liquor. One boarding master was bringing off five or six men in a small boat which was nearly capsized several times before reaching the ship.

After all the men got on board, the second mate came along and roared out : " All hands lay aft to the quarter deck and answer to your names." The men managed to get aft somehow, some so intoxicated that they could scarcely stand. The chief mate came

12

with the ship's "articles" in his hand and commenced to call out the men's names, in the presence of the captain and boarding master. As several of the men had deserted other ships which were still lying in Australian ports, they were obliged to ship under fictitious names, which some of them had actually forgotten—one man in particular who had signed on under the name of Johnson. He was a big, sulky-looking Scandinavian, who was half drunk at the time. The mate called out "Johnson" several times and received no answer. The boarding master, who was standing near the mate, became so enraged that he up fist and laid the man out on the deck. "What is your name now," he roared out. "Yonson," said the man.

This procedure over, the towline was passed to the tug, the ship was unmoored and we started to tow out to sea. The second mate roared out : "Lay aloft and loose the sails." About seven of us went aloft and started loosing sails, while the others went into the forecastle. The second mate rushed after them and tumbled them out on deck, some of them head foremost. The man who was loosing the foretopsails along with me remarked that the second mate was a bully to all appearances, when he started manhandling men so early in the voyage. Those who were able to go aloft crawled up somehow, drunk and all as they were, but three men were scared to leave the ship's deck, and we found out later on that they were not sailors at all. The second mate gave each man a thrashing, but that could not induce them to leave the deck.

We found out afterwards that one of our men had deserted an Orient Liner in Sydney, and had been a "Jimmy Ducks" on that vessel. Another was nothing short of a cut-throat, a mongrel from the Southern States of America, half-Mexican probably, known as a greaser in that country. The third man said he had been a Sundowner in New South Wales.

We all could see that we had got on board a red hot ship and that we would have to move around pretty lively. The sails were set by steam, and the officers and bos'n were bawling out continuously : "Here you, on the foretopgallant yard, look alive and overhaul the foretopgallant spilling lines, damn you." "Now then,

you Hobo on the main crosstrees, overhaul the main royal buntlines." The weather was fine, with a light breeze from the south-
west, and as soon as all sails were set we hauled in the towline,
and the towboat came alongside to wish us a pleasant voyage, which
was another way towboat captains had of asking for a bottle of
whisky. This is the usual way towboat captains have with ships
outward bound. Our captain was a Nova Scotian and told the
skipper of the tug to go to Hell.

This was a Clyde-built ship, but commanded and officered by
" blue noses " (Nova Scotians). The captain was a man somewhere about 45 years of age, and had the reputation of being a
tyrant. The mate would be about ten years younger, and the
second mate would have been about thirty. They were expert
officers and seamen, and expert knockers-out, as all Nova Scotians
had the reputation of being in those days. The second mate was
in every sense a bully, wore a red shirt, a bucko cap, and a huge
gold ring on the little finger of the right hand, which could do
service as a knuckle-duster as well. He had an evil look about
him, and it is certain that if he had lived in the days of the old
Buccaneers he would have excelled in that profession. We found
the chief mate, on the whole, to be very just when he found a man
anxious to do his best, but woe betide the man who was lazy, or
did not move around fast enough, or was inclined to be saucy. I
was in the first mate's watch, and although I was young and
inexperienced, in marline-spike work especially, he treated me well
for a man of his calibre.

After the tug left, and sails were properly set, we were sent to
dinner, which was composed of beef and potatoes—two potatoes
for each man and about a quarter of a pound of beef as tough as
leather. At eight o'clock that evening watches were picked. The
mate first picks the man he thinks the best; the second mate then
makes his choice; then the mate again, and so on until the crews
are allocated in watches. The most useless-looking men are the
last to be picked.

The mate, before dismissing us, informed us that the watch on
deck must stop on deck and under no circumstances go into the
forecastle during their spell of duty. No one was to sleep on deck,

and when an order was given from the quarter deck by an officer or bos'n, it must be repeated in a loud voice by the watch on deck. No lamp was allowed to burn in the forecastle after 8.30 p.m. All hands, except the man at the wheel and the man on the lookout, were to muster on the quarter deck to answer to their names at eight bells. The second mate then stepped forward and informed us that when eight bells were struck he wanted the watch below out on deck flying. If there was any hanging back, we would find him outside the forecastle door with a greenheart belaying pin.

My first trick at the wheel was at midnight. The wind had hauled to the south-east, and the man whom I had relieved gave me " by the wind," which meant to keep the ship as close to the wind as she would lay. He also whispered to me that the captain had been up a few minutes before and caught him a point or so off the wind, and swore at him, saying also if he caught him off the wind again he would get the whole roof kicked off his skull.

People living on shore can only have a hazy idea of the stern discipline which prevailed on sailing ships of those days, and this one in particular, where a man could not call his soul his own. There was no afternoon watch below; all hands had to be on deck working during the afternoons; on Sunday the decks had to get a special clean. Sweating up halyards and sheets with watch tackles followed. The old Western Ocean song came in true here :

"For Sunday's devotion there is watch-tackle drill,
For it goes to their hearts to see you stand still."

After a couple of days out, it was quite evident that, in addition to hard work, and hard, exacting captain and officers, we were in a starvation ship. So one day we decided to go aft and ask the captain for more food, as it was impossible to keep soul and body together on what we were getting. Aft we all went, and asked the steward to see the captain. The steward went into the saloon and stated that the men were aft demanding more food. When the captain came out of the saloon and saw all hands there waiting on him, he demanded to know what was the matter with the food. A man by the name of Wilmot, who was the spokesman, asked him how men could possibly work on the food we were getting :

maggoty biscuits and coffee for breakfast, which was nothing but hogwash; a small piece of meat and two potatoes each man for dinner; tea and maggoty biscuits for supper. The captain demanded to know what we wanted, as we were getting what the Board of Trade allowed us, and we were not entitled to any more. We informed him we were not getting our Board of Trade allowance, and we would demand to see it weighed out. "Wall," said he, "you are quite welcome to see your food weighed out."

Next day two men went along and saw the meat weighed out, but when it was cooked it was less than ever. The meat had been weighed out all right, but the full amount had not been sent to the galley. The living was as poor as ever, potatoes were bad, and in order to keep ourselves alive we were obliged to pound up the maggoty biscuits—maggots, weevils and all. The biscuits were put into a canvas bag and pounded on the iron mooring bitts with an iron belaying pin until they were as fine as flour. Scraps of salt beef or pork were shredded fine and mixed up with the biscuit meal and baked in the galley oven. This mess went by the name of cracker hash. Sometimes the biscuit meal was mixed with treacle water and baked in the oven until it somewhat resembled gingerbread; then it went by the name of dandy funk.

It was apparently the captain's intention to pass through the Cook Strait, but on the second day after leaving port a strong southerly buster came up along the coast, which made it necessary for us to pass north of New Zealand. The southerly buster was very strong, and although the yards were almost on the backstays we were averaging twelve knots with royals and upper topgallant-sails fast.

The captain, in addition to being a man driver was a ship driver as well. When passing the Three Kings the wind hauled to the south-east and freshened up almost to a gale, the ship ploughing through it with the lee rails in the water, and sending the spray, sometimes, as high as the foreyard. All hands were called out and ship had to be snugged down to reefed upper topsails and full foresail. This occupied all hands about six hours. The port watch was sent below at 3 a.m. I turned into my bunk as I stood up, with seaboots and oilskins on, expecting to be called out again at any minute, and in any case at 4 a.m., when it would be my watch on deck.

We were called at a quarter to four.   I had the misfortune to fall asleep again, though my watch-mates apparently were under the impression that I was awake.   When watches mustered on the quarter deck the men's names were called out as usual, and I was found to be missing.   The second mate came along and, shaking me roughly, informed me that as I belonged to the mate's watch he would leave it to the mate to deal with me.   I was accordingly brought up on to the poop to where the mate was standing, when I was told by that gentleman that if this offence happened again I would have to stop on deck three watches in succession, and that I could thank my lucky stars for getting off so leniently.   He also added that his reason for letting me off so easily was that he had noticed that I could move around and seemed to be anxious to do my best.   The captain suddenly appeared on the poop and inquired what was wrong.   The mate informed him that I had slept in and had to be called by the second mate, adding at the same time that he was letting me off owing to the way that I performed my duties.

The captain then turned round and asked why I had slept in. I informed him that I was tired and sleepy, and happened to drop off.   " I guess," said the captain, " that we make no allowance for the like of this here.   It may be human nature to fall asleep, but human nature is not going to have its own way in this packet; cast-iron discipline will be maintained here, for this is no ordinary lime juicer.   You must understand that everyone of you belongs to me, body and soul, while you are in this ship; you are under orders, signed articles, to obey, which plays havoc with your own private opinions, and if you fail to hear the watch called, you being tired and sleepy won't excuse you.   I will not have an officer going and tapping you gently, and asking you to get up if you are not too tired to do so."

I remarked that I was sorry, but still at the same time I considered this a very hard ship, where a man could not call his soul his own.   The captain replied that the ship was commanded and officered by Nova Scotians, men who were not afraid to give an order, not like the ordinary English officer who was afraid to let himself be heard, but went bleating around the decks like a wether in the lambing season. " I guess," said he, " there are no easy ships or easy places in this world for men who wish to get on. I myself went to sea at the early age of 14 on board of a New Bedford whaler, where the belaying pin was judge, jury and sometimes executioner, and I have by hard work climbed the ladder to where I am.   Now, beat it."

SOME OF MY SHIPMATES.

OUR crew was a mixed lot : nine Britishers, one American, two Swedes, one negro, one German, one Greek, and one Chilian.

There was also the bos'n—an Irishman by the name of Farley, who had been a voyage in the ship. He had about as dirty a disposition as the second mate, but was unable to carry it out to the same extent. He was on duty all day chasing the sailors around.

The sailmaker was a German and was always seeing what he called spirits, but spirits of the wrong kind, he said—they were departed spirits or ghosts. He said the other kind of spirits would not annoy him, as he was always prepared to take a double whack of them. The spirits that he saw sometimes used to sit on the bench beside him. He said that they were mostly old men and women whom he had never seen in life. In other respects he was quite sane, and a good seaman as well as a sailmaker.

The cook was a Manxman—little Hughie we called him—a man about 50 years of age, and one of the survivors from the London. This vessel, of about 1700 tons burden, owned by Wigram & Sons of London, was a full-rigged ship with auxiliary power equal to 200 horse-power, which foundered in the Bay of Biscay in January, 1866. The cause of the disaster was through heavy seas breaking on board and smashing in the engine-room skylight, which had a glass top. The water poured down into the vitals of the ship, and as the crew were unable to stop this inrush of water, the vessel sank in a few hours, and out of the large number of passengers and crew there were only 19 survivors.

This is a good illustration of how lax the Board of Trade were in those days, to allow a ship to proceed to sea with so many lives on board, with an engine-room skylight only about five feet above the waterline when the ship was loaded. Engine-room skylights and fiddlays of modern steamers are never situated near the water.

The carpenter, or Chips as he was usually called, was a big, hefty Swede, who was thoroughly master of his trade.

There were several elderly men among the Britishers, one of the oldest being a man by the name of Jim Miller, from Dundee, who had had a long experience as a boundary rider up country on the large sheep and cattle stations. He was a man of about 50 years of age, and a splendid seaman. He informed us that he was at the Ballarat gold rush when he was only 20 years of age. After having a fairly good run of success he came down to Melbourne to have a good spree, and bought all that part which is now Port Melbourne, blew the rest of his money, went back to Ballarat, and fought at the Eureka Stockade, got badly wounded, and had to go to hospital in Melbourne, got better and shipped on a vessel going to London. He happened to be in New York shortly after the Civil War broke out, joined the American Navy and served under Farragut down south about New Orleans. After the Civil War was over, he eventually drifted back to Australia after an absence of several years, tried to claim his property, but had no title or document to prove that he was the legal owner, and consequently lost it.

Next to Jim Miller was an American, who stated that his real name was Billy Barton, a native of the State of Massachusetts. He was the son of a shipmaster who had commanded several of the American packet-ships running between Liverpool and New York. Those ships, without exaggeration, were floating hells. The men who manned them were known by the name of Packet Rats, mostly Liverpool Irishmen, and Irish Yanks. Every officer had to be a fighting-man, and as desperate as the sailors were. The knife was always in evidence and murder was quite common in those ships. Officers were always armed with a belaying pin stuck into their seaboots, knuckle-dusters in their pockets, and very often a gun in the hip-pocket. After leaving port all sheath knives were taken from the men and given to the carpenter to file the points off the blades. Forecastles at the same time were searched thoroughly in case there were any more knives about, or offensive weapons of any kind. Officers never had stand-up fights with sailormen, as they considered that put them on the same level as the men. Handspike hash and belaying-pin soup were terms used in those packet-ships, and were considered very stimulating in getting a move on.

During the process of shortening sail in those ships, captains have been known to luff the ship up in the wind so that the flapping sails would knock the men off the yards. The writer once met a business man in New York who had been a passenger on board a packet-ship and was an eye-witness to the ship being deliberately luffed up into the wind so as to shake the men off the yard when they were reefing a topsail; but fortunately the men managed to hang on. This gentleman also informed me that the mate of this particular ship always carried a blackjack in his sleeve, which he used most unmercifully on the men's heads. One man was killed during a storm on the Banks of Newfoundland. The mate killed him on the quarter deck with a handspike, picked him up, and tossed him over the rail. The whole business was treated as a joke next morning at breakfast.

All bullies are considered cowards, but such was not the case with the officers in those ships; they were desperate men, and without fear. Steam launches used to meet the ships off Sandy Hook to take off any officer who wanted to clear out for a little while. When an officer had killed a man he generally slipped on board one of those launches and went in hiding until the ship was ready for sea. He generally joined her again as she was outward bound, going down the harbour. The mate, who took the place of the officer who was in hiding, was known in those days as the " Sweetener." He was always a fine man, and the ship got a good name in port. As the ship was towing down New York harbour, he slipped ashore in the same steam launch that brought the original mate back.

Those were the kind of ships that Billy Barton sailed in under his father, who was commander. He must have had a splendid training in the art of handling turbulent men. He left the American ships and joined the British " Black Ball Line," out of Liverpool. He joined as a junior officer and eventually rose to chief officer of the crack " Black Ball " liner called the Lightning, under the celebrated Bully Forbes. By all accounts the Lightning was a fairly hot ship. One night when coming to anchor off Williamstown, a negro gave Barton cheek, or to use his own words, " gave sass," which was more than Billy could stand, especially from a nigger. Billy picked up a handspike and immediately laid the nigger out with it. The blow was so heavy that he considered the nigger was dead. He reported the matter to Bully Forbes, and explained that he was to clear out right away. The night was dark and blowing fresh, with a choppy sea. A boat with four men in it rowed to Sandridge and landed Billy there sometime about midnight. Bully Forbes gave Billy the address of a friend up at Ballarat whom he could rely upon. Billy bought a horse from a cabman and rode away for Ballarat, where he found Bully Forbes's friend.

A few days after his arrival at Ballarat he received a letter from Bully Forbes asking him to return to his ship, as the nigger came round all right and deserted his ship on the following night. The letter also stated that the four men who put Billy on shore at Sandridge were never seen again, but the boat was found on the beach. Billy, however, had caught the gold fever, and made up his mind to stay on the goldfields. He stated that he had a fairly good run of luck, and, as was the usual way with miners in those days, after having good luck they went down to Melbourne to have " a good time," as they called it. Miners were always recognised by the old slouch hat and moleskin trousers tied below the knee. Many of those diggers had been seafaring men, who still had a liking for the sea, sailormen, and ships. There was always a possibility of meeting old shipmates, and then things did hum. Those sailormen-diggers were lavish with their money wherever they went. In a public-house it was their rule to shout for all present, no matter how many were standing at the bar. Their favourite recreation was to drive round Melbourne in a two-horse vehicle with flags flying, and one or two fast ladies along with them, singing " Rule Britannia " or " Reuben Ranzo " at the top of their voices.

During Billy Barton's first stay in Melbourne he reckoned that he got through nearly a thousand pounds in less than a month. It happened that Jenny Lind, the Swedish Nightingale, paid a visit to Melbourne, and Billy went to a theatrical agent and booked a seat in the dress circle. When the house was full, Billy marched to his seat in his miner's rigout, the old slouch hat, moleskin trousers, coarse chequered coat, and hobnail boots all covered with clay just as he left the mine. There was quite a commotion when Billy sat down amongst some of the most fashionable people in Melbourne, who were all in evening clothes. The manager of the theatre appeared on the scene and tried to persuade Billy to leave the circle, but he stoutly refused, stating that he had paid for his seat and there he was to remain. To get even with the theatre-going people he went to the theatrical agent next day and bought the whole dress circle out for £350, and sat there by himself in his mining rigout. Many years afterwards I met some people from Ballarat who knew Billy very well, and they assured me that this story was quite true.

Billy returned to Ballarat after I was shipmate with him, and was receiving good money out of mining investments. He had not been to sea since leaving the Lightning until he came with us. He evidently was well-off then, but apparently the sea was calling him, and he was so pleased at the looks of the graceful ship that he decided to make a trip in her to his native country, but to use his own expression, he " had reckoned without his host."

The oldest sailorman of all was Old Alick, a Londoner. He had fought in the American Civil War under General McLellan at Antietam, and later under General Grant. He was a fine old man and must have been a splendid soldier in his day. He must have been nearly 60, as he said he intended to remain in the United States owing to his war pension being due.

Macpherson, the Scotsman, was a man of about 35, as strong as Sandow, a splendid sailorman, and from his own account, a hard drinker. He had been working ashore in Sydney some time before this when he answered an advertisement for two keepers who were wanted to go to England in one of the Orient Liners in charge of a lunatic. Mac and a friend of his took on the job for fifty pounds each, as they wished to pay their passages out to Australia again. This lunatic was a sailorman off some ship who was debarred from remaining in Australia by the New South Wales Government. Mac made a particular study of the man's temperament, as he considered it might come in handy for himself some time. The man was quite harmless, but he had a mania for fishing; he would sit on the top of a deck-house for hours with a broom handle for a fishing rod, a piece of spunyarn and an old rusty nail for fishing tackle.

When Mac got to England and handed the man over to the proper authority and received his fifty pounds, he made up his mind to book his passage out in the same steamer as he came home by, but unfortunately the best laid plans of mice and men aft time gang agley. Mac had been a total abstainer for a considerable time, but on the day on which he received his pay he bought a new suit of clothes and went to the theatre in the evening—to the Queen's in Poplar—and when there he and his mate had a few drinks with some ladies who frequented that place, one of whom decoyed him to some house and robbed him. His Highland blood was up, and when a Highlander sees red he is a tough man to deal with. He gave the woman a thrashing, and also the two bullies who probably picked his pockets, smashed up furniture, and gave the policeman who arrested him a beating up. The result was thirty days with hard labour.

When Mac came out of prison he had to go to the strawhouse —a shelter for hard-up sailors. He managed to get a pier-head jump at Gravesend in a barque bound for Sydney. On the passage out, when near Australia, Mac started the insane dodge, and started fishing in the same manner as the lunatic who was under his charge on the passage to England. Sometimes he would be at the wheel and call out to be relieved as he had to go and fish. As soon as he got relieved he would get on the forward deckhouse and sit with his legs dangling over the side of it, with his broom handle and string, with a rusty nail for a hook. The captain of the vessel apparently became very anxious, as it meant the man would have to be sent to England, which would be a heavy expense on the ship. Mac did not fish every day, as that was a part of the game he was working. On the day before arrival, the captain (who was a young man newly promoted) asked him if he would like to go fishing after arrival in Sydney. Mac said he would, as he was a born fisherman.

On the day after arrival in Sydney the captain sent for Mac and asked him if that was one of his fishing days. " No," said Mac, " but I feel it coming on me again. I expect I shall be fishing to-morrow again." " Come to the shipping office," said the captain, who was glad of the chance to get rid of him before he took one of his peculiar turns. As it was very unusual for captains to pay off sailormen at that season of the year when wages were very high, there was just a possibility of the shipping master getting suspicious. The captain had to caution Mac in case any questions were asked by any of the officials. Mac was paid off in due course before a junior clerk who asked no questions. About a week or so afterwards, the captain met Mac and asked how the fishing was getting on. " Oh, I'm no fishing the noo; I did good fishing when I fished the money due me, and my discharge; that wass verra good fishing, captain."

Mac had been a policeman in Mauritius before that. He was several mcnths there before he had a case, and that was the inspector, whom Mac arrested one dark night when he was drunk. He was severely cautioned after this, but he got drunk again, and had to be taken to the police station on a wheelbarrow or hand-cart. This ended Mac's career as a policeman.

After being ashore a while in Sydney he got out of employment and very hard up, so hard up that he had to sleep on the domain. He said that he could always get plenty of drink from old acquaintances, but no food. When he shipped with us he had been starving, having lived on beer the whole time. When he did get any money from anyone to buy food with, it was always converted into beer. It was out of the question trying the insane dodge in the ship we were in, and Mac never entertained the idea.

Cockney Charlie was about 32 years of age, and the smartest seaman on board. He was really a child of the sea, and had been at it since he was a boy of 14. He was a very powerful man, and no man on board could stand the hardships we had to endure like him; he never seemed to get tired. He neither drank nor smoked, and although an expert boxer he never cared about lifting his hand

c

to anyone unless in self-defence.   He had been in Devitt & Moore's ships all the time, in the Australian trade.

Little Taff was a whisky-guzzling, drink-sodden little Welshman, and could never keep sober when drink could be obtained.

Wallace, the negro, hailed from Baltimore, and was a white man in every respect, except in colour—a hard-working, good-tempered, steady man.

Finnigan was a Liverpool-Irishman from the vicinity of Scotland Road, Liverpool; a tall, thin, wiry man and a fairly good sailorman, but rather nervous up aloft taking in sail.   He came on board drunk, in Newcastle, and was one of those who was thrown head foremost out of the forecastle by the second mate, whom he never forgave for that insult.   He happened to be in the first mate's watch and did not have a chance of testing the second mate's qualities as a fighting man until later on the voyage.   One day Finnigan and Cockney Charlie nearly came to blows, but as Charlie was a quiet man, nothing took place.   When Finnigan got out of temper he used to always slap his chest and exclaim, " I am a Scotland Road buck, that is me, Joe.   My father was a Western Ocean packet rat."   He would then get up and pace the deck and say to himself after slapping his chest a few times, " That's me, Joe.   I'm a dandy, I am.   I'm a law unto myself.   God help the skipper or mate that gets athwart my hawse.   They don't know Finnigan in this here packet yet."

The man we called the Greaser we found out to be a regular " stiff " from the Bowery in New York.   He was no use as a sailor, as he could not leave the deck.   He was a thin, sallow-looking individual, which indicated that he was a halfbreed of some kind with all the vices and none of the virtues of the two or three races from which he had sprung.   Owing to his dirty habits he was flung out of the forecastle, and had to sleep in the donkeyroom.   The second mate gave him the boot several times, until he eventually stabbed the second mate.

Jimmy Ducks was a little Cockney out of one of the Orient Line steamers and was unfit to go aloft, but was very anxious to do his best on deck at odd jobs, such as holystoning and scrubbing paint, chipping iron rust, etc.

Jimmy " Know-all," whose right name he said was Noall, was an ex-Navyman, and not much of a sailor except at knotting, splicing, grafting, etc.

Williams, the Sundowner, was no sailor either; he managed to crawl aloft as far as the lower yards, but no further.

The rest of the crew were all fairly good sailormen and had no particular idiosyncrasies worth mentioning.

A HURRICANE—AND AFTER.

AFTER passing north of New Zealand we had fairly good weather until abreast of the Low Archipelago, when we ran into the tail-end of a hurricane. The first indications were about 2 o'clock in the afternoon when the sky became overcast, and about 3 p.m. very threatening. Then the captain gave orders, "All hands shorten sail." Luckily the wind was light from the south-east, and we soon had the ship snugged down to topsails and foresail. All hands were then sent to tea, about 6 p.m. The wind was still fairly moderate, but the ship was plunging heavily into a head sea, taking the water green over the bow at times.

We had scarcely finished our tea when the vessel was struck by a terrific squall right abeam. The chain foretack carried away, and the lee foretopsail sheet. At the same time the foreyard cockbilled, the weather yard-arm going up to the topsail yards. The ship went over with her lee rail in the water. The foresail, fore lower topsail, inner jib, and fore topmast staysail all split and went to pieces in two or three minutes' time; the noise they made was like a whole battery of artillery going off at once. Topsail halyards were let go, but owing to the ship lying over so far, the yards would not come down the mast. The rain came down in torrents, at the same time lightning was blazing about in all directions and the sea was tumbling on board all over the ship, with men, ropes, and everything moveable floating about the decks. Luckily no one was washed overboard.

In less than ten minutes no sails were left standing except the main lower topsail, nothing being left of the other sails but bolt-ropes. Whole clouds of canvas were seen floating in the sea to leeward. The ship was still lying with her lee rails in the water, which made it quite evident that the coal cargo had shifted. Owing to the roaring of the hurricane, and the thunder also, it was impossible to hear an order, or even move around the deck owing to the sea coming over in cascades.

28

The second mate came and bawled into my ear : " Go and relieve the wheel." I had to go hand over hand along the weather poop-rail, and then crawl across the deck to the wheel. Harry, the Greek sailor, who had been at the wheel, had lost his head, and was calling on all the saints in the Greek calendar. The captain bawled into my ear to take the weather wheel, and let the Greek go to the lee side and help.

The sea was now breaking on board over the poop also. One heavy sea took the port cutter off the top of the forward deckhouse, and stove in the port side of the starboard cutter. After I had been about ten minutes at the wheel, the wind hauled almost right astern. We commenced to gather headway, and after a while the men on deck managed to get the yards squared in.

During this process, which took nearly an hour with the whole crew on to the braces, the ship was swept almost from stem to stern by one enormous wave which broke in over the starboard bow. The doors on the front of the poop were smashed in and the saloon almost gutted out, pig pen with four pigs went over the side and could be seen floating for some time afterwards. The chief mate was washed along the deck nearly the whole length of the ship from the fore rigging to the break of the poop, and had to be carried into his room with a broken collar-bone. The jib-boom carried away shortly afterwards, and with it the fore topgallant mast snapped over and came down about the men's heads. Old Alick, the A.B., had two ribs broken. The ship still had about 10 degrees of list through the cargo having shifted. The wind was now howling from the south-west, and no sail was left standing except the main lower topsail. When the yards were squared in we had the wind right aft and went along about eight knots under the main lower topsail. All hands were now sent to clear away the wreckage of the jib-boom and fore topgallant mast.

About midnight, when everything was secured, orders were given for all hands to lay aft for grog, which rather surprised us all. The steward served out the grog in the saloon, and gave each man what may be called in nautical parlance a double whack.

As the ship was still lying over with a heavy list to port the order was given : " All hands get into the hold to trim coal," so as to get the ship upright.   The wind was still howling and right aft, so the trimming of coal over to starboard was more necessary than bending sails.   At two o'clock in the morning coffee was served out, and at 4 a.m. the steward came below with a tea kettle full of rum and lime juice, diluted with water.   " Here you are, boys," said he ; " drink my health ; you can see that I am not the mean whelp you all take me to be.   When I treat men, I treat them liberally."   He was quite aware that we had no use for him, and that we considered that he was largely responsible for our poor living.   We could see that he was nearly drunk when he came down into the 'tween deck.   Little Taff got a hold of the kettle in case the steward capsized it, and up went the spout into his mouth, and if Cockney Charlie had not jerked it out of his hand he would have been drunk in a few minutes.   A pannikin was brought below and each man helped himself according to his appetite or carrying capacity.   In less than twenty minutes Macpherson was thrashing the Greaser.   Little Taff was lying dead to the world.   Billy Barton and Jim Miller were trying to fight, but could not stand up.   In a very short time all hands were drunk except Cockney Charlie, Wallace the coloured man, and myself.

The bos'n reported to the captain that nearly everyone was lying dead drunk down in the hold among the coal, owing to too much rum being put into the tea kettle.   When the captain came down into the hold he started swearing.   " Wall," said he, " this beats election.   Here is a ship nearly on her beam-ends with her cargo shifted, scarcely a rag of sail set, completely at the mercy of wind and sea, and the crew all drunk."   He tasted the contents of the tea kettle.   " Suffering cats," he exclaimed, " this stuff in this here kettle has got quite a kick in it.   No wonder the men are all drunk.   There has been enough rum put into it to intoxicate three ships' crews."

The second mate came down to see how things were getting on. (He had been having a sleep and the bos'n keeping watch.)   As soon as he saw the captain he knew something was wrong. " Look at this," said the captain.   " That worthless, rotten-to-the-core hobo of a steward has mixed this here dope too strong, and now nearly all the men are soused with rum; all their back teeth must be awash."

Macpherson was trying to sing " My Nannie's Awa," when the second mate gave him a kick, which acted like magic. Mac was about sober in a minute, and anyone could see that his Highland blood was up. " You got tam blue-nose," he cried. " You kick me, will you; kick a man when he is down and trunk." Mac made one rush at the second mate and caught him by the throat and flung him among the coal. The second mate got up and swayed unsteadily on his feet, trying to study the roll of the ship and catch Mac unawares. Watching the swing of the ship he made a rush at Mac. The blow he aimed missed Mac's face by a few inches only. Mac's counter, helped by the roll of the ship, sent the second mate sprawling among the coal again. The second mate gathered himself together for another onslaught, but Mac punished him severely with clean, hard blows. The second mate was getting very groggy and leaden-footed. He made another rush at Mac and clinched, but Mac loosened the clinch and caught him with a short left below the chin followed by a swinging right to the face, which laid him out again.

The captain now interfered, and told the second mate to go and keep his watch. The drunk men were brought up on deck, and they all made for their bunks. No more work was done until ten in the forenoon, when we started to bend sails—the weather being quite fine again. We could see that the second mate had received severe punishment from Mac, and he was still looking very groggy.

When the captain went up out of the hold he found the steward speechless drunk in the storeroom and the rum barrel rolling all over the place empty. The rum was washing from one side of the storeroom to the other. The steward had undone the lashings, which resulted in the barrel getting adrift.

Fine weather prevailed and sails were bent in the place of those blown away, and the ship was trimmed upright. The broken jib-boom and fore topgallant mast were not replaced until our arrival in San Francisco.

The thrashing which the second mate received from Mac had a very salutary effect on him. The steward, by all accounts, received a thrashing from the captain, and the consequence was there was a marked change on the amount of food we were getting. Some of the men remarked that when rogues fall out, honest people come into their own. Personally, I think that the captain took no hand in cheating us. I blame the steward for the short weight; the man, beyond doubt, was a crook.

We were now practically four hands short, with Old Alick being laid up with two broken ribs, and the three hobos, who were of very little use on board. Under these circumstances it came very hard on us. The second mate felt quite taken aback after the rough handling he received from Macpherson down in the hold; he was an entirely changed man for a few days. Finnigan, the Scotland Road buck, was itching to have a slap at him. He reckoned that if Macpherson was able to get away with him, it would be an easy matter for Finnigan himself to knock him out. Finnigan knew that he could not very well be the aggressor, as the punishment is very severe for striking an officer; but with a man of the second mate's temperament, it was an easy matter to make him take the offensive.

One afternoon Finnigan got an opportunity of getting his own back. We were unbending the mainsail, and Finnigan was slacking away too much on the weather reef tackle. The second mate shouted out "Hold on the weather reef tackle." Finnigan paid no attention, but kept slacking away. The second mate roared out "Hold on to that reef tackle, you Liverpool ———." Finnigan immediately took a turn of the reef tackle round a pin, walked over to the second mate and asked him to repeat those words over again. In less than a second the second mate shot out his left on to Finnigan's right temple, followed by the right, which laid him out like a flying jib downhaul. After lying on the deck for more than a minute he got up and made a rush at the second mate and clinched, but the second mate being a much stronger man had Finnigan at his mercy and threw him off and landed him on the deck with a dull thud. Finnigan got up again, but one swinging right to the jaw settled him. Finnigan was a very tame man after this experience, and no one was sorry for him, as forecastle blowhards are, as a rule, disliked by their forecastle mates.

The usual rains, calms, and variables were experienced in the doldrums. After getting the north-east trades the weather became very settled. One Sunday when we were doing only about four knots we noticed quite a large number of sharks following the ship. This is considered to be a bad omen by some seamen. When a shark follows a ship they say that someone is going to die, and that the shark is waiting for the body. Some of the foreign members of our crew still held to that opinion, but the Britishers had no superstitions of any kind.

The shark-hook is made out of a piece of steel about three-eighths of an inch thick, with about three feet of chain on to it, because a shark can bite a piece of rope over easily. One large shark was keeping close under the counter all the time with a pilot-fish just a few feet ahead of him. The captain granted permission to the men to come on the poop to try and catch this big fellow, which was about eleven feet long. As shark hooks do not have barbs on them the piece of pork must be tied on to the hook very securely. A tail-block is made fast about thirty feet up the main topgallant backstays; a rope is rove through this and brought to the taffrail, so that as soon as the shark takes the bait the men haul up and get his head as high out of the water as possible and take a turn around the taffrail. The rope from the backstays now comes into use, by making a running bowline around the rope which the hook is attached to and slipped down around the shark until it is as low as his tail, when it is tightened up. The men at the main rigging now tail on to this rope, and the men at the taffrail slack away on the hook-line so that the shark is hauled up into the main rigging tail uppermost, and then landed on deck. As soon as he touches the deck he makes a fine old row for a while. One man rams a handspike into his mouth, and the carpenter comes along with his axe and chops his tail off. The tail is fixed on the jib-boom end as a rule, and the stomach is examined before he is thrown overboard. When a dead shark is thrown overboard the others do not eat him.

As we were nearing the Mexican coast a very large dolphin was caught one day—large enough to make a meal for all hands. Little Hughie, the cook, boiled him, and after he was boiled he guaranteed him to be quite safe for eating, as he had a shilling in the pot which came out as bright as when it was put in.   This is the test for deep-water fish, which are sometimes poisonous; a piece of silver, or silver coin, is put in the pot along with the fish, and if found to be discoloured the fish is not fit to eat.   Some of us scarcely tasted the fish, and others made a hearty meal and were poisoned.   The poisoning is not of a very serious kind; the face becomes swollen, the eyes seem to get small, and the sufferer has a severe headache which lasts for about twenty-four hours in the worst cases.

During the latter part of the voyage fine weather and light north-east trade winds were experienced.

ADVENTURES AT FORT SAN DIEGO.

THE small lighthouse outside Fort San Diego was sighted on our sixty-first day out. At eight o'clock in the evening we were off the harbour entrance, but as the wind fell away light, and off the land, we had to lay the ship with her head seaward and dodge about until daylight. No one on board had been at this port before, but the prevailing idea amongst many was that it was a bad place for yellow fever, especially during the wet season.

The Union Jack was hoisted for a pilot, but no one came off, and the captain found it advisable to anchor in the outer part of the harbour. The Yellow Jack (quarantine flag) was hoisted, and we then had to wait until the afternoon before anyone came off to give us pratique—that is, permission to go on shore. As soon as pratique was obtained a pilot came off and brought us inside, where we were to discharge our cargo.

Fort San Diego is a very old town, and in the days when the Spanish galleons made this the port where they landed their treasure from the Phillipine Islands, it was a place of some consequence. The treasure was taken across the Isthmus of Darien and transhipped to Spain. The harbour of Fort San Diego, which is fairly large, can accommodate quite a large number of vessels, and the inner part of the harbour is well sheltered from all winds. A few American steamers used to call there—about one in every ten days, if I remember rightly. About two thousand tons of our coal cargo was for this port, for coaling steamers; the remainder, twelve hundred tons, was for San Francisco.

The town of Fort San Diego at this time was in a state of decay, and had probably a population of about two thousand of a mixed race. The only prominent building was an old fort going fast into ruins, a part of which was used by Guardias Rurales (Rural Guards), and another part as a prison for all kinds of malefactors.

President Dias was the Dictator of Mexico in those days, and was the only Dictator who was ever able to rule that country in a satisfactory manner. For twenty-one years his iron hand guided the destinies of Mexico and made it a fairly prosperous country, but after his death the country was the scene of insurrections and revolutions for about twelve years. Presidents were set up against walls and shot, one after another; brigands were everywhere; and there was no security either for life or property.

The old fort held a fairly large number of prisoners, some of whom had spent over twelve years in it, and had never been tried or sentenced. The military prisoners had been court-martialled by their commanding officers and sentenced in the usual way, but the civilian prisoners seemed to be forgotten.

A few months before our arrival in Fort San Diego the bos'n of an American ship called the Indiana shot the chief mate dead, and was taken on shore and left in the military prison. He had no idea when he would be tried before a judge. The military authorities said it was no business of theirs; they seemed to take a liking to the prisoner and treated him very well. The Indiana at the time was discharging coal at a rate of over two hundred tons per day, which was more than any other ship managed to discharge, and yet the captain and mate were not satisfied. The mate went down in the hold and struck the bos'n with a shovel. The latter, in self defence, struck the mate on the head with a piece of coal, which so enraged the mate that he told the bos'n that he would shoot him and made a rush for his cabin to get his revolver. The bos'n also ran for his, and both men met in the 'tween deck and commenced firing at long range. After the exchange of two or three shots the mate fell mortally wounded.

As there was neither a British Consul nor an American Consul anywhere near Fort San Diego, the bos'n managed to get word sent to the American Minister at Mexico City—the capital of Mexico. The American Minister passed it over to the American Consul-General in that city, who stated that as the man was a British subject his case lay entirely outside of his jurisdiction, and that it was a matter for the British Consul to take up, and passed it on to that official. The British Consul made strict investigations, but saw that he could not interfere as the man committed the murder on a foreign vessel. He promised to refer the matter to the Foreign Office in London, however. If the man could prove that he was actually British-born, and had never taken out American citizen's papers, he stood a good chance of getting fairplay.

In Fort San Diego the hard, dirty work is done by Chilians and negroes. The Mexican does not believe in hard work of any kind, and he must always have his afternoon siesta. The health of the port was good during our stay there; the heat was very intense during the day, but it was fairly cool at night. We had very little sickness of any consequence, except what was caused by some of the men drinking a native drink called pisco—a native brandy.

When the ship had been secured in her discharging berth and cargo gear rigged, all hands were ordered into the hold to shovel coal. According to the articles of agreement we could not refuse to work cargo of any kind, but we had all made up our minds beforehand that no cargo would be touched by us unless we received substantial food to keep us up to the work in such a hot climate, where the temperature was sometimes as high as one hundred degrees in the shade.

Upon the order being given for all hands to shovel coal, we all marched aft and demanded to see the captain. The second mate went into the saloon to inform the captain that all hands wished to see him, and after a few minutes he came out on the quarter-deck demanding to know what was the matter. Cockney Charlie was selected as spokesman. He informed the captain that we were all quiet men and were not looking for trouble of any kind, and those of us who were sailormen had proved ourselves to be first-class sailormen in every respect. We had been practically four men short during the whole trip owing to Old Alick being laid up with broken ribs, and three of the hands shipped in Newcastle were useless hobos who could not leave the deck to go aloft. During the storm encountered on the passage, when the sails were blown away and the ship was almost on her beam ends with the cargo shifted to one side, we proved ourselves to be supermen.

"Waal," said the captain, "what to Hell is all this long-winded sermon about anyhow.   Boil it down and get to the point; what do you all want?"

"We want to know," said Charlie, "if we are expected to work this coal cargo out on the same starvation food we have been getting since we came on board.   If we are, we refuse to go down the hold point-blank."

"You are not going to dictate to me," said the captain.   "If you refuse to work, ashore you go to jail right now."   And turning on his heel, he ordered the second mate to run the police flag up for the Vigilantes to take those men ashore to jail.   On hearing this, we all went forward to the forecastle to get ready for going to jail.

The chief mate was now able to get about, and we all noticed a look of disgust on his face when the order was given to put the police flag up.   We all could see that he was in sympathy with us, and we naturally expected some developments.   The second mate, again, seemed to be only too glad to see us all sent to jail.

About ten minutes afterwards, the second mate came along and roared out "All hands lay aft on the quarter-deck."   When we reached the quarter-deck the captain and his officers were waiting to receive us.

"Now men," said the captain, "I want to make a start, and if you work well, you will get more food, and if you do not work to my entire satisfaction, to jail you go.   So get into the hold right now."   The scowl seemed to have gone off his face, and we moved towards the main hatch and went below and started work.   The digging down and shovelling of coal under a blazing sun was terrific work until we got well down and under the deck.

Hughie, the cook, was aft for stores and he overheard a heated argument between the captain and chief mate.   The latter was in entire sympathy with us.   He told the captain that no man could work hard in a climate like that of Fort San Diego with the food we had been getting, and that he himself would not do it if he were one of the men.   After a heated argument the captain agreed to order more food for us.   After we had made a fairly good start we lived like fighting cocks while we were working cargo.

The second mate, however, had it in for Cockney Charlie, and one day the two men had words which resulted in blows, when the second mate got knocked out. Although he appeared to be the stronger man of the two, and was a much heavier man than Charlie, after a few minutes anyone could see that he was no match for his opponent, who had twice his endurance and was an expert, clean fighter. The second mate fought as long as he was able to stand up, and when he saw that he could not stand up any longer to his opponent, he stated that he had had enough, as his eyes were almost closed up and the bridge of his nose was broken. No one was sorry for him except Charlie himself, who actually sympathised with him, which showed the kind disposition of the man.

Several of the men had made up their minds to desert, but they soon found out that Fort San Diego was no place for a white man. The pilot, who was a Chilian, kept a shop and supplied ships' crews with provisions, such as eggs and fruit of various kinds. The captain paid the bills and had the usual commsision. The amount of the bill was kept off the men's wages, who purchased the goods.

The first Sunday in port was an unusually cool day, and we all went aft and asked the captain for permission to go on shore. He was quite civil, but stated that he could not grant this request owing to the risk of some of us getting sick and being unable to work when we returned. He, however, promised us a day off once the cargo was discharged, one half of the crew at a time.

Several of the boys were getting a thirst on, and one night an Indian passed with his canoe close under the bow. Little Taff had a few shillings left, which he gave to the Indian on condition that he would bring off a bottle of pisco. After a while the Indian returned with the liquor, and Taff, Finnigan and a Norwegian were soon drunk and rolling about the decks.

The discharging of the cargo proceeded rapidly, and as soon as it was all out the port watch was sent ashore on leave. This happened to be on a Sunday. Seeing Sunday was not a working day and did not count, we were allowed Monday as well. On Sunday morning when we all went on shore the first place we made for was the pilot's shop, where we made arrangements for a good dinner. Cockney Charlie, Jimmy " Know All," and Billy Barton had a desire to go and see some place about fifteen miles in the interior called the Cave of Bad Winds, where a great battle had been fought. The pilot took them to a man called Pedro of the Mules, who agreed to take the three men out for two Mexican dollars apiece. Pedro spoke good English, having served as a steward on the Californian coast.

As Fort San Diego was an old ramshackle place there was nothing worth seeing, so some of us went up to the fort to see the man who shot the mate of the Indiana. The pilot took us up and we had no difficulty in seeing the imprisoned man, who was allowed to go all over the place, but could not get outside past the sentry. The prisoner told us his name was Frank Ford and that he was a native of Greenock. The soldiers, he said, treated him very well and he received the same rations as they did. Although at first they were not civil to him and called him a Gringo—a name they have for Englishmen—seeing he had killed an Americano they gradually took to him and called him Señor Franko. Frank said that he regretted killing the mate, but he had to do it in self-defence, because the mate went up for his revolver with the full intention of shooting him. The captain, before sailing, gave him a letter stating that he, the captain, quite recognised that the shooting was done in self-defence, and that he would make a full report on the matter to the proper authority upon arrival at the first American port.

Frank had a cell-mate, an officer of the Mexican Army, who had been tried by court-martial and received three years' imprisonment for insulting his commanding officer. He and Frank were on very good terms and he took his regular turn in cleaning out the cell. There was a soldier in a cell near by who had been condemned to be shot for killing a non-commissioned officer. The time of his execution was fixed for daybreak on the following Tuesday morning.

After having a good dinner at Spring-heeled Jack's (the pilot told us that was the name he went by to the crew of the last English ship which called at that port), we took a walk in the country, returned to Spring-heeled Jack's, and had supper, and went on board again at nine o'clock as tired as if we had been shovelling coal. The men who went up country in Pedro of the Mules's coach did not return that day. Next day was Monday, which was our proper leave-day. We went ashore again, and all returned in the afternoon except two, and the three men who went up country.

Next morning we had to turn to, and the other watch went ashore on leave. The men who went up country were still absent, and it became evident that something had happened to them. After breakfast the captain went ashore to get someone on their track. Spring-heeled Jack was sent away to look for them, and returned with the men next day. When Spring-heeled Jack went up country he found all the four men in jail. One of the Rurales (Rural Guards) reckoned that Pedro of the Mules was a notorious horse-thief of long standing, and that the three sailormen were partners of his, and consequently the whole four men were arrested as horse-thieves.

The prison was a house with a shingle roof and an adobe wall. The jailer was full of pisco all the time, and the three sailormen considered this a good opportunity to dig through the adobe wall (which was nearly all composed of clay) with their sheath knives. Pedro, however, begged them to leave it alone as they really had committed no offence and could not be kept in much longer. After being nearly twenty-four hours without food, they commenced hammering and kicking the jail door, which eventually aroused the jailer from his drunken sleep. There was a small porthole on the door where the jailer looked in and demanded to know what all the noise was about, and if he was to be deprived of his siesta by a lot of noisy gringoes. The men in reply demanded food. " If you want food," said the jailer, " you must pay for it, because we never feed horse-thieving gringoes or marineros here for nothing." Billy Barton handed the jailer five Mexican dollars through the porthole. " This is not enough," said the jailer. " I want another five dollars, and two more dollars for myself."

After receiving seven more dollars he went away, remarking that he would be back with food in less than an hour's time. One hour passed, two hours passed, and still no food. The men commenced hammering and kicking the door again, and after a while one of the Rurales put his face to the porthole and demanded to

D

know why all the noise was being made. If the men made any
more noise he threatened to go in among them and bayonet them.
The men informed him that they gave the jailer twelve dollars
over two hours ago to go and buy food with, and he had not
returned. " Madre de Dios," exclaimed the Rurale, " you should
have had more sense. The jailer will be blind drunk for several
days now, and will never return so long as he has a centavo left.
Give me ten dollars and I will find an honest man who will go and
get you food."

After making a tarpaulin muster the men managed to raise
seven dollars among them. " No bueno," roared the Rurale, as he
slipped the money in his. pocket, " I must have ten dollars or
something valuable, in addition to the seven dollars." Whilst
casting his eyes around he noticed that Cockney Charlie had a
watch. " Hand me over the watch also, and I will be able to get
you some food." Charlie stubbornly refused to hand his watch
over, as he considered the Rurales were a parcel of rogues.

The Rurale blew his whistle, and in a few minutes five or six
Rurales came marching along to the jail door with fixed bayonets.
The door was opened, and three men marched inside to plunder
the sailormen, whilst the other Rurales stood ready with rifles
and fixed bayonets. The men were searched thoroughly and
relieved of everything of any value; even their coats and hats
were taken away.

The men were now in a dreadful state of mind. They expected
to be starved to death, and were in a small cell with scarcely any
air except what came from the porthole in the door. They had
nothing to sit or lie on except the bare floor. They had been
locked up on Sunday evening and had received neither food nor
water. The room was infested with large poisonous spiders called
tirantulas, and poisonous centipedes. They shouted and hammered
on the door, but no one seemed to take any notice of them. Night
came again and they tried to sleep, but the fear of being bitten by
the tirantulas and centipedes kept them awake most of the night.
Pedro of the Mules was almost in a state of collapse, as the men
blamed him for being a crook and the cause of all this trouble
being brought on them. They searched him and took his knife

from him as a necessary precaution, in case he went mad and killed them all in the dark. Pedro called on Santa Maria and nearly all the saints he could think of, to bear witness that he was an honest man and never stole anything in his life.

When the men had been locked up about forty-eight hours without food or water, a Rurale looked in through the porthole and told them that if they did not keep quiet he would let some air into their bread-bags with his bayonet, and throw them out afterwards for food to the buzzards and alligators.

On Tuesday afternoon they heard a commotion outside of their door, which made Pedro of the Mules shout out " Viva practico Juan Amigo Mia," which Billy Barton repeated many a time afterwards. Pedro recognised his friend the pilot's voice outside the door and knew that they would soon be released. One of the Rurales soon afterwards opened the door and told the men to clear out.

It appeared that Spring-heeled Jack, the pilot, informed the Chief of Rurales that the men were English sailors and strangers in the country, so also was Pedro of the Mules to a certain extent, he being a Chilian and had only been a few months in the country. Pedro demanded his two mules and coach, and the officer of Rurales gave orders to bring them along. The messenger returned with the coach and one mule only. The other mule, he stated, had bolted shortly after the men were arrested, and consequently Pedro was a poorer but wiser man. Spring-heeled Jack, the pilot, bought food for the men, and engaged another man to bring the sailormen down to the port in his coach, which they did not reach until nearly midnight. After a tedious night-journey the men returned to the ship tired and hungry, and unfit for work that day.

The captain informed them that as they had overstayed their leave, the time off duty would be kept off their pay, and all expenses incurred by the pilot for bringing them down country and back to the ship would also have to be made good out of their wages.

The men when they were driving up country noticed a swamp with an alligator about sixteen feet long lying stretched across the road where they had to pass. This made it necessary for them to turn back and get on to another road. They observed that many of the inhabitants were piebald.   The natural colour of their skin was dark brown, but they had large white patches all over their bodies, which made them look like a piebald horse.   Those people are called pintos in Mexico, which means piebald; a piebald horse is called a pinto in Mexico.   Those pintos are lepers.   The leprosy is caused by eating alligators, and unlike the other leprosy in other parts of the world it does not as a rule prove fatal.   When an alligator kills an animal he does not relish the carcase in a fresh condition.   He leaves it until it is quite putrid.

The Mexican is considered to be the finest horseman in the whole world, and is said to pass nearly half of his lifetime in the saddle; even the beggars are sometimes found on horseback.   When ashore on leave I saw Mexicans breaking in a horse.   One man rode into a corral where several horses had been newly brought in, and lassoed a very fine animal by one of the hind legs.   He then took a turn round his saddlebow, which gave the captured horse a severe fall.   Another man, as the horse was about to fall, threw a lasso around his neck; a large bit fixed on to a large rawhide bridle was pushed into his mouth.   The man who was to ride him was standing by with a large sheepskin saddle, while two other men tied the horse's legs together.   The saddle was placed on his back, girth straps tightened up, and when everything was ready the man put one foot in the stirrup, the horse's legs were loosened, the lassoes were taken off, and the horse went plunging and rearing around the corral with the man on his back.   The horse ran forward, backward, sideways, and tried every manoeuvre he could think of to unseat the rider, and after a quarter of an hour he became exhausted and perfectly cowed.

ON PASSAGE TO SAN FRANCISCO.

NO desertions took place in Fort San Diego, and twenty-four days after our arrival there we set sail for San Francisco with the remainder of our coal cargo.

The second mate had been fairly quiet in port, but we were not many hours at sea until he commenced bullying again. He started on the rookies first. Jimmy Ducks and the Greaser were sent to shift the main topmast staysail over the main stay and hooked the lower block on to the pennant instead of the double block. The second mate on seeing this, thrashed the two of them most unmercifully. On the following day he got on Finnigan's track, and knocked him down. None of us had much sympathy with the Greaser, as we all knew that he was a bad article; and as for Finnigan, he was very unpopular, being a bully also if he could get away with it. But poor Jimmy Ducks had all our sympathy. He was a harmless and willing little chap, and although he could never be a sailor, it was not his fault.

Shortly after Jimmy Ducks had received his thrashing from the second mate, McPherson found him crying like a child in the forecastle. We happened to be coiling up ropes on the quarter-deck just before eight bells when we saw Mac. coming from the forecastle with his sleeves rolled up. It was evident he was seeing red; his Celtic blood was up and his war-paint was on. He walked straight up to the second mate and held his fist to his nose. " Look here, you Nova Scotian hound," he said, " I have a good mind to break every bone in your body. If you put a hand on that little Jimmy Ducks again I will beat you up into a pulp. Now that is my first and last word. Look out!" The second mate seemed thunderstruck and never opened his mouth, and Mac. went away forward to the forecastle.

That evening I asked the Greaser how he felt, as I noticed one of his eyes was closed up. For answer he came out with a whole string of Yankee oaths—to be more explicit, Bowery oaths.

45

" Look here," he said later on, " I am going to croke that second
mate. You'll see, now. Mark my words, I have croked as good
a man as he is before now. He is a big powerful man, I admit,
but I shall take no chances. I shall make a clean job of it when I
am at it."

" Are you meaning what you say " said I. " Or is this all
bravado on your part? If you kill the second mate, as you say,
mind it will be an eye for an eye, a tooth for a tooth, and your life
for his."

" I guess I shall wait until we get to 'Frisco," said he, " when
I can do a clean job and get away at the same time. There is no
stabbing in the back with me. You run the risk of striking a bone.
The neck is where I always aim at with a downward stroke."

I came to the conclusion that this was all " hot air " with this
loathsome piece of humanity, who had not the courage to defend
himself with anything when he received the thrashing from the
second mate. I took no more notice of him and did not mention
the matter to anyone. About a week or so afterwards this
rapscallian of a man tried to kill the second mate when he was
coming forward along the deck one dark night. The carpenter
was sitting in his room and noticed the man passing his door with
a knife in his hand, which he had been sharpening that forenoon
in the carpenter's shop. The carpenter pretended to have gone
to bed, but sat up instead to watch the man who was moving about
quietly, like a cat. Shortly after ten o'clock the second mate was
heard coming forward along the starboard side of the deck. The
would-be murderer let the officer go past the donkey-room where
he was concealed, and then slipped after him with hand raised
ready to strike the fatal blow. The carpenter bellowed out " Look
out, mister." The second mate made a jump to one side when
the knife came down and struck him in the shoulder-blade with a
downward stroke. The man raised his hand to give a second blow
when he was jerked backwards by the carpenter from behind so
suddenly that he fell flat on his back on the deck, and the knife was
taken from him. All hands were on the spot in less than a minute.
The man was dragged aft to the quarter-deck, where he was hand-

cuffed and leg-ironed round a teakwood pillar and kept there for most of the passage.

The wound in the second mate's shoulder was about three inches long. Though only a flesh wound, it was necessary for him to go to hospital in San Francisco.

The passage to San Francisco was uneventful, and on the twenty-third day out we sighted the Farrallon Rocks about thirty miles from the Golden Gate. Two tugs were seen coming out towards us, and by the smoke they were making, we came to the conclusion that they were racing for all they were worth. We had a fine leading wind, and the captain made up his mind to sail right into the harbour without taking a tug. As the tugs drew nearer to us we could see that one of them seemed to fall behind the other very quickly. The faster tug came up close alongside (her name was the Racer) and hailed us. Her captain offered to tow us in for 350 dollars.

"Three hundred and fifty hells," roared our captain. "Do you think I am mad," said he.

"Waal, no," said the captain of the tug, "I don't think that, but the wind will come off the land before long, and it will be a heavy pull to drag a big ship like yours against it; and the ebb tide will be strong when we near the harbour entrance."

"I will only give half of that amount," said our captain. "The wind will stay to the westward all this day, and in any case I am not in a hurry to get in, as we shall have to wait a while—I should say about two months—for this season's grain, so what is the use of paying you or any other towboat man an extortionate rate for towage when we shall have to lie doing nothing for two months, and the ship eating her freight up in wages and provisions. I guess we would get aground on our beef bones."

"Say, cap.," said the towboat skipper, "I guess you are a Bluenose, and I would bet my bottom dollar that there is not much fear of any ship that you are in command of getting aground on her beef bones, as I always find that ships commanded by Nova Scotians are the most starve-gutted vessels on God's earth. Waal, seeing that you are a Bluenose, I cannot expect to make expenses out of you, so I will reduce my charge to three hundred dollars."

"Waal, now," said our captain, "that is a small concession. I will raise my figure to two hundred dollars, which will be my last word. By saying two hundred dollars, this is to include the use of your towrope and all harbour removals."

"That ain't no good," said the skipper of the tug. "Good-bye," and with that he left us and steamed seaward, I presume to look for another ship.

The other tug came alongside shortly afterwards and offered to tow us in for two hundred and eighty dollars. "Nothing over two hundred dollars," said our captain. "The wind is fair, you know, and we can sail right up to our anchorage." The pilot cutter was only about five miles away, and orders were given to haul up the mainsail, and stand by to back the main and crossjack yards. About half an hour later we backed those yards for the pilot.

American pilots I have always found to be a fine class of men, and the pilot we took on board was one of the best. As soon as he came on board he advised the captain to take a tug, as the wind would most decidedly come from ahead before long. "What rake off are you going to get from the towboat people for persuading me to take a tug, eh, pilot?" The pilot felt very insulted at this remark made by the captain, and replied : "It is no business of mine, captain. I am here to advise you. Make your own arrangements."

About half an hour later we were braced sharp up on the port tack, and not long afterwards the wind shifted right ahead, but fairly light. The tug was still close by and on seeing the shift of wind he came back and offered his services, but the rate was now increased to three hundred dollars owing to the wind being ahead. The wind increased off the land, night was coming on, and negotiations between the captain of the tug and our captain were at a deadlock, which resulted in the tug leaving us to steam away seaward. The wind remained fresh off the land all night, and on the following day the captain had to pay two hundred and seventy dollars to get towed in to the anchorage, where we dropped anchor at five o'clock in the afternoon.

Our anchor was scarcely down when we were surrounded by boats, the majority being boarding-house runners' boats to take the men out of the ship. The chief mate ordered the boats away from the ship's side until the vessel was properly moored, the sails made fast, and the decks squared up.

After the ship was properly moored with both anchors down, the chief mate gave orders to lay aloft and furl the sails. As I was stepping on the sheer-pole to go aloft on the fore, the chief mate called me to where he stood on the forecastle head. "Look here, son," he said, "lots of things will happen on this ship to-night. Now, mind you do not taste drink, which will be handed on board by the landsharks who are alongside now. Do not be fool enough to desert your ship. I want you to keep night-watch while the ship is in port, so go now and get your tea and then keep watch."

I felt quite elated that the chief mate had taken a kindly interest in me, seeing that he was a man of very few words. When he gave orders they were rapped out in a sharp, incisive manner, and lately everyone liked him, being at the same time afraid of offending him. Instead of going aloft, I went to the galley to get my tea, and when I returned I found two boarding-house runners and three sailors in the forecastle.

The boarding-house runners were treating the sailors, who were at the same time giving an account of all the hardships and starvation which we had to endure. "Never mind, boys," said the runners, "that is all at an end. You are in this here Golden City of San Francisco where everything goes easy. Why, even the ducks fly tail foremost to keep the sun out of their eyes. The girls greet you with a smile on the streets, and old sailor million-aires treat you every time they meet you. Gee! isn't it some place! We don't believe in the pace that kills here."

The other rascal came over to where I was sitting having my supper of hard biscuits and tea, and demanded to know what was the matter with me. "Gee!" said he, "why are you not packing up and coming ashore with us? Have a smile—it is real old Kentucky whisky. Don't drink any more of that strike-me-dead tea, it is only hogwash and not fit for any man to drink. And those Liverpool pantiles, what your owners call biscuits, are only sweepings of the bakehouses with some lime or whitewash put in to help to whiten them."

I declined to sample his real old Kentucky whisky, stating that I preferred whisky made in my own country. " I guess you are Scotch," said he, " and as narrow-minded and as close-fisted as the rest of your countrymen." I noticed that he had still some indications of the low German gutteral in his throat, which made me ask him if he had been long in America. " Why, sure," said he, " I am an American and was born in Noo York." I contradicted him and told him that he was a Squarehead, and some of the sauer-kraut could still be seen between his teeth.

When the sails were all furled and the decks squared up, all hands were sent to tea, and I had to go on duty. Several more boarding-house runners came on board and made straight for the forecastle. I suppose each man had his bottle of chain lightning, which never failed to have the desired effect, for when Sailor Jack gets a glass or two in, everything appears in a new light to him. What was a good ship is then a bad one ; good captains and officers are the worst afloat until he goes on another ship, when he changes his mind again. The last ship is then always a good ship, with plenty of grub, captain and officers all gentlemen.

As I was standing near the forecastle I heard one of the runners making a long speech to the sailormen. " Men," said he, " it gives me great pleasure to meet you all here this evening, and in the name of my employer, Mr. Pete Gallagher, I invite you to his house, where you can stay as long as you please. There is a free bar in the house, and you can get a good rig-out of clothes when you leave. There is dancing in the house every night after nine o'clock. We, of course, will find you dancing partners. It so happens that Pete has several empty rooms owing to a run on his men all of a sudden. Let me see, now—oh, yes—six men left to go as bar-tenders up country."

" By Jingo," said a Swede, " your house for me." " And me," said his mate, another Swede. And both men started packing up. " That's right, men," said the eloquent one. " And now, I may also state that there are several vacancies on Pete's list for other jobs. Four men will be wanted in a week's time for shifting scenes in a theatre, and we have vacancies for bar-tenders off and on all the time, the wages ranging from twenty to thirty dollars a week, and all found." "I am going with you," said the German. "Sensible man," said the runner. Little Taff was drunk and was ready to go with anyone.

"Now, men," continued the orator, "if any of you are fools enough to go to sea again, of course, we can get you a job. I have been to sea and know what it is. I would not send a dog to it. It is a sorry day for me when I have to take men—excuse me!—fools, I should say. I say again, I feel sorry when I have to bid good-bye to men who are going away on a long voyage such as to Europe somewhere." At this, the tears actually rolled down his cheeks, and he stopped speaking for a few minutes. One of his mates gave him a drink, and he started off afresh. "Now, again, men, I say if any of you are fools enough to go to sea again there was an American yacht captain applying to us for ten able seamen who will be wanted in ten days' time. She is going on a long cruise in the Pacific. The wages are forty dollars a month and uniform."

At nine o'clock that evening all had deserted except four of us, viz., Billy Barton, Cockney Charlie, the Greaser (who was in irons) and myself. Even Old Alick and Jim Miller changed their minds when they tasted the runners' whisky. Little Taff, Finnigan, and Jimmy Ducks were put over the side in a bowline and lowered into the boat, owing to their being dead drunk. I found out afterwards that six of those men were taken straight from our ship to an American ship which was waiting for a crew. The name of the ship was the Gatherer, a vessel with an evil repute, which could never get a crew except by shanghai'ing men. There was a captain and mate in her who were sentenced to long terms of imprisonment. The mate apparently had a political pull, and got pardoned when Grover Cleveland became President of the United States. He was still living in 1912, and was then a very rich man in San Francisco, having made a fortune as a stevedore and in other ventures in which he was interested. The Gatherer was towed to sea shortly after the men were hoisted on board. Three months' wages went to those crimps who took them out of our ship—most probably the one with the soft heart who could turn the water-works on like a water tap.

I met one of the men in London about three years afterwards, and he informed me that although the ship had a bad repute, the captain and officers in her at that time were not too bad. She made a quick passage to Havre, and his pay-day only amounted to a couple of pounds. The other men who deserted were only two days ashore when they were sent away in a Liverpool ship bound to Falmouth for orders.

It seems very strange that Great Britain should have been the leading maritime nation of the world over a century or more, and never exerted herself in the least on behalf of her seamen who visited ports in the United States. The nefarious business of crimping flourished in every United States port. The commanders of foreign ships were set at defiance by those crimps, who had politicians and judges to back them up. They would take a whole ship's crew out of a ship in broad daylight right before the captain's eyes, and defy him, even threaten to shoot him. A man is persuaded to desert his ship by plausible scoundrels, and sent away a day or two afterwards with three months' advance. Some of those crimps and boarding-house keepers were very rich men.

Great Britain had not the courage to protest against the crimping of her seamen in American ports. Protesting may have been useless owing to the outcry which would have been made by those rascals who lived on the earnings of British seamen. In America in those days every crimp had a strong political pull, and his political boss came in for a large share of the proceeds derived from this business. At all the large seaports the crimps had a strong organisation for their own protection.

Mr. Havelock Wilson of the British Seamen's Union went across to America about twenty-six years ago to investigate the state of affairs, and to see if nothing could be done to upset this three months' advance business in sailing ships. He visited several of the British Consulates, and he saw that crimps were allowed inside one Consulate when men were being paid off. Mr. Wilson reported this on his return to London, and after a considerable time the advancing of three months' pay was declared illegal, and according to the new American law a man could only receive one month's advance.   There was an outcry among the crimps, who styled themselves shipping agents.   " We must have the money, our lawful money, which we are entitled to.   We shall not supply sailormen to any vessel for a bare month's advance." The consequence was that they demanded twenty-three dollars as blood money in New York; and in San Francisco they demanded as much as seventy dollars as blood money for each man.   This blood money eventually came down as low as ten dollars for each man.

SAN FRANCISCO IN 1884.

WE berthed at Oakland Wharf on the opposite side of the harbour to San Francisco. We received a visit almost every evening from the crimps, with the object of persuading us to leave. According to their version, fortunes could be made in a very short time in San Francisco.

One day three runners came on board when we were at dinner. " Hullo," said Cockney Charlie, " have you come on board for a feed? " " Oh, the Saints preserve me from eating dog's meat," said one of them, who was an Irishman. Another of them took a biscuit out of the bread barge, split it open with the point of his knife, and, sure enough, there were several large maggots. " Suffering catfish," he roared, " look at this ; nothing but hogs could eat this ! Look here, boys, are yues mad? Why sit here and eat lobscous, buffalo beef, mutton—half dog and half sheep? Pack up your dunnage right now and come with us. Jobs are to be had anywhere. Your old shipmates struck it good, some of them. The young Swede is now a bar-tender in the Palace Hotel, fifty dollars a month and all found. The nigger is away up country rigging scaffolds at no less than sixty-five dollars a month, and here are yues sitting eating food that I would not give to my dog. Have a drink right now and pack up."

" Look here," said Cockney Charlie, " you get out of this. If you want to keep your craniums whole, get out of this forecastle before you are thrown out."

" Who would throw me out? " said one.

" I would," said Charlie, jumping up to his feet at once.

The crimps had no wish to get into a row, and one of them tried to calm matters down. " Look here," said he to Charlie, " I guess you can handle yourself, and you are just the right kind of man I am looking for to go as a sparring partner to Spud Welsh. I could also get you a second mate's berth on one of our American ships bound to Noo York."

Charlie sat down and took no more notice of them. The mate came along and turned the men to, and the boarding-house runners went away without any success.

The second mate's wound was slow in healing up, and it was found necessary to send him to hospital. The Greaser was tried at Court and sentenced to six months' imprisonment.

Billy Barton deserted, and informed me before he left that he was taking train to the Eastern States, which was his intention when he came on board.

The boarding-house runners paid us another visit on the first Sunday morning after our arrival and introduced the bottle of good old Kentucky to the bos'n and sailmaker with good results. Both were decoyed on shore and were never seen again so far as I know. They had been about nine months in the ship, and must have had a lot of money due them. The sailmaker was a harmless kind of fellow, but the bos'n was a very disagreeable man, and no one was sorry to see him take his departure.

The crimps paid little Hughie, the cook, a visit occasionally, but he always told them that there was nothing doing.

All deck hands had now deserted except Cockney Charlie, the carpenter, and myself. Charlie was employed at the sails most of the time, and I was night watchman. We received good food after the crew had gone, and the ship had been quiet after the second mate was laid up.

San Francisco in 1884 was considered to be the wickedest city on the face of this earth. Sodom and Gomorrah were nothing to it, and I think that the only bright spot in it was the British Mission to Seamen. People in this country have only a very hazy idea of the amount of good seamen derive from those institutions, which are found in every large seaport in the world. As soon as a ship arrives the missionary comes on board and invites everyone, from the captain to the deck boy, to the institute. Young apprentices derive no end of benefit from places of this kind : these boys are ignorant of the wickedness of a place like San Francisco, and need the fatherly help of such men as Canon Kearney or Mr. Hardy of Valparaiso, whose names used to be familiar to every British seaman on the Seven Seas.

Were it not for those institutions, men would spend their time and money strolling round the town and frequenting dives and dance houses. These institutes are controlled by the Church of England, and the seafarer can spend happy evenings at all kinds of games, such as billiards, bagatelle, draughts, boxing, and gymnastics. Concerts are given about twice a week, and religious services are held twice or three times every Sunday. Very good teas are served for a few cents only, and a few men can be accommodated with a night's lodgings. Although the institutes are controlled by the Church of England, no attempt is made to ram religion down one's throat; every man is made welcome, whether he be Roman Catholic, Hindoo, Mohammedan, or Buddhist.

During Mr. Kearney's time in 'Frisco, crimping was at its worst, and it has been often said that the crimps dreaded going near a ship when he was on board. He was known as the Fighting Parson, and I have no doubt that many of them have felt the weight of his sledge-hammer fist. He was transferred to 'Frisco sometime about 1894. I met him in Buenos Aires about 1912, when he was known as Canon Kearney. To look at the man one could see that he was a born boxer; it seemed to be his hobby. Seamen all over the world know him by repute as the Fighting Parson and Sailor's Friend.

The discharging of our coal cargo proceeded very slowly at Oakland Wharf owing to so many ships being in the port with the same kind of cargo. Our sails were unbent by shore riggers, the master rigger being an Inverness man by the name of John Campbell—a man who had had a varied career. He went to sea as boy and worked his way up to chief mate, had an ordinary master's certificate, left his ship on the west coast of South America when Chili and Peru were at war, joined the Peruvian Navy as a bluejacket, served under Admiral Grau in the Huasco, and was alongside the conning tower when the Admiral was killed. Campbell was eventually taken prisoner by the Chilians and released when the war was over. He beat his way up to San Francisco and worked at various jobs. After working around the water-front for a couple of years he seemed to get tired of casual jobs and wanted something more permanent.

The policemen seemed to get rich very quickly, so Campbell made an application to get into the force.   After passing a medical examination he was summoned before the official who made the appointments, and was informed that as the position was a very profitable one he would have to pay a sort of entrance fee, which ranged from three hundred to six hundred dollars.   It was really a bribe to the official.   If the new policeman paid the six hundred dollars his beat would be a very lucrative one.   The policeman who brought the most money to the chief rose very quickly in the force, and he always had the best money-making centre, *viz.*, the streets which were known as the tender-loin or underworld of the city, where the gambling houses and brothels were.   Campbell only paid the three hundred dollars, and was sent on duty on the water-front, which was considered the worst beat in San Francisco. He was in the police force about two years.   The cold eye of his superior officer was always on him, and as he was put on the carpet every now and again, it soon became apparent that he was not wanted there.   Consequently he resigned.

Being out of a job, he went as a longshoreman, and when working on board a vessel commanded by an old shipmate of his who persuaded him to contract for rigging work which had to be done on that vessel, he made his first start at what turned out to be a very successful business.   He informed me that the police force in San Francisco was reeking with corruption all through. All the dance houses, gambling houses, opium dens, low drinking saloons, dives, cocaine-joints, brothels, professional assassins (now called gunmen), etc., had to pay heavy bribes to the police, from the chief down to the constable.

I was in California many years afterwards when the mayor of San Francisco was brought before the court for being the owner of several gambling dens and houses of ill-fame.   He was supposed also to have raked in nearly a million and a half dollars from contractors.   The trial fizzled out.   The State of California is full of stringent laws, all made to be broken.   Law-breakers who accumulate enormous sums of money always boast of owning

E

those whose duty it is to enforce the law, and are known as the Vicious Circle which can always be squared. Those same law-breakers who have become wealthy often have several lawyers drawing retaining fees in case they are needed. Some of the large trusts in America are reputed to have twenty or more lawyers drawing retaining fees.

After keeping night watch for about ten nights I was quite delighted one day when the chief mate told me that I was to go on day duty again to assist Cockney Charlie at sewing sails. Keeping night watch is considered to be a job for an old man who is not able to go aloft. The riggers painted the ship outside, and after the sails were all repaired, Cockney Charlie and I painted the masts and spars, which was a big piece of work for two men. A night watchman was brought from the shore, some friend of the captain's who had probably fallen on evil days.

Charlie and I were advanced five dollars every Saturday night, so that we were able to go and see the sights of San Francisco. Campbell, the rigger, as well as the seamen's missionary, told us the parts of the town we should keep clear of. Although they advised us not to go near Chinatown, curiosity got the better of us and we went there one Sunday, and were disgusted with the unwholesome smells of chop suey, sharks' fins, birds' nests, and dried octopus, which came from the Chinese eating houses. The streets were narrow and the houses were all of the Chinese style. We seemed to be in the heart of China all of a sudden. Western civilisation seems to have a very bad effect on the average China-man. The men whom we saw in Chinatown all had a vicious look about them—murderous, repellant looks. Charlie and I walked through two or three streets, but declined to enter any of the houses. We went to have a stroll through one of the public parks instead, and had a splendid tea at the Institute on our way back to the ship.

On the following Sunday Charlie and I were invited to spend the day at a Mr. MacDonald's house. Mr. MacDonald was a friend of Campbell, the rigger (both from Inverness), and had been over twenty years in San Francisco engaged in the lumber trade—a partner in a large sawmilling firm. He had a fine residence in the suburbs, and was very Americanised, I suppose owing to his wife being an American. He had five children, the oldest being about sixteen. His wife and family showed very bad taste when they expressed their anti-British opinions to us.

The children in America become very anti-British when they start going to school. Their teachers and history books make a very false impression on their young minds. They look upon the people of Great Britain as a decadent race, suffering from dry-rot, and entirely lacking in initiative. They are more or less slaves, crushed under the iron heels of a monarch and arrogant nobility. The men who would not submit to this tyranny came to America in the Mayflower, and a similar kind of men come to America yet. George Washington, with a mere handful of backwoodsmen, rounded up whole armies of Englishmen. Paul Jones, another great hero, mauled the British Navy wherever he met them. The fight between the Shannon and Chesapeake was the only time that the British had a look in, and that was because the Chesapeake was shorthanded. Tyranny prevails wherever the British flag flies, and the British persecute the black inhabitants in the countries which they conquer, and then try to civilise them with the Bible in one hand and rum in the other.

I consider that American school history books should be revised entirely, so that the children of that country may grow up with a better feeling towards the average Britisher.

The Americans always had a friendly feeling towards the Irish, and to the Scotch also to a certain extent, but not so to the English, whom they looked upon as being full of snobbery and conceit and with no business capacity. Cockney Charlie and I swore that we should never go back with Campbell again to see his American friends.

When our cargo was all discharged down to four hundred tons, which we needed as stiffening to stand up with when shifting ship, we towed across from Oakland Wharf to Long Bridge Wharf, where we took in four hundred tons of wheat. We then discharged the remainder of our coal.

AMONG THE "CRIMPS" AND WAITING FOR A CREW.

WE left Long Bridge Wharf early one Sunday morning for an anchorage in the bay. As Cockney Charlie and I expected to have Sunday alongside the wharf, we felt very disappointed at having to remain on board all day. As the new crop of wheat was still coming down very slowly, we fully anticipated that we should lie in the bay at anchor for two or three weeks. Lying at anchor out in the bay was very monotonous as there was no chance of getting on shore.

One day the chief mate roared out " Lay aft, you two men, and get the boat out; come along, quickly." Being at dinner at the time, we dropped everything and ran to the boat falls. " Get into the boat you two men, and Chips and I will lower you into the water." On looking aft we saw what was the matter. A boat under sail had capsized and was close under our stern, and four men were hanging on to the gunwale. The wind was blowing half a gale at the time, and quite a sea was running. The chief mate intended to slack us away with a long rope on to the boat's painter so that we could reach the upturned boat without getting adrift ourselves. Charlie and I shipped an oar each and backed our boat astern while they slacked away on board of our ship. About ninety fathoms of rope were slacked away before we reached the capsized boat, and after a considerable amount of difficulty we managed to get three of the men on board our boat, but the fourth man weighed about eighteen stone, which made it impossible for us to do anything with him. He was half drowned also, and was on the point of letting go his hold. We managed to get a small piece of rope round him which we made fast to the stern sheets of the boat, and thus prevented him from drowning.

The chief mate, carpenter, steward, night watchman, and cook all tailed on to the rope and hauled us up to the ship, and when we lay in the calm under her stern a rope ladder was put over, but none of the rescued men was able to climb it. They even had the audacity to ask the mate to put one of our lifeboats over and go after their boat which was drifting up the harbour. The big fat man was still in the water and on the point of collapsing. I noticed that he had a large bottle in his inside coat pocket, so also did one of the other men whom I identified at once as the eloquent one who could shed tears when parting with sailors. It was quite evident that they were all crimps or keepers of sailors' boarding houses. As they were all dripping wet and shivering with cold, the mate lowered a rope's-end over the taffrail with a bowline on it, and ordered them to get into the bowline and climb up the rope ladder at the same time.

After the three of them got on board, Charlie and I got a rope round the fat fellow, who was now almost dead. It took eight men all they could do to get him on board. After he was stretched out on the poop deck, I noticed a look of disgust come over the mate's face. "Who is this man?" said he. "I seem to have seen his face before." One of the men said that the gentleman was a Mr. Franklin, one of the principal citizens of San Francisco. "I guess," said the mate, "that he is Shanghai Franklin, the greatest crook unhung in San Francisco; I remember him very well. He has been piling on the fat since I saw him, like all the rest of his kind."

As soon as Franklin was brought on board Cockney Charlie treated him as the apparently drowned are treated. The mate ordered Franklin's three confederates to get busy and get heat into that big mass of flesh, and give him a drink out of his own bottle. Cockney Charlie got hold of the bottle and was in the act of pouring some of the liquor down his throat, when he put his hand up and pushed it away, and one of his friends jerked it out of Charlie's hand remarking that Mr. Franklin was a total abstainer.

"You three men look very cold," remarked the mate, "you cannot be abstainers also; have a good drink to warm you up," and making a rush at the same time snatched the fat fellow's bottle from the man who held it.

Cockney Charlie took the other bottle from one of the three men. "Now, drink," said Charlie, "or else I shall pour it down your throat." The man refused point blank to taste it even.

"The dirty stuff is doctored," said the mate. "I have a darned good mind to pour it down your throats right now."

The three men admitted that the stuff was doctored, and that they were making for a Liverpool ship a few cable lengths ahead of us, and in trying to pass across our bow they got foul of our cable and lost their rudder; the boat capsized and drifted along our starboard side, and their yells drew the mate's attention. If the mate had not heard them, the career of four of the worst rascals along the water-front—especially Shanghai Franklin—would have been at an end.

Campbell, the rigger, knew all about him when he was a policeman around the water-front. He had shanghai'ed a French-Canadian priest in the Glory of the Seas, bound to Havre. He had admitted that he had often shanghai'ed dead men, hauled them up the ship's side in a bowline, remarking to the mate of the ship that the man was drunk, but he could vouch for him as being a good man when he was sober. He, like a great many other boarding-house keepers, kept a drinking saloon, and, what was called in those days, a "free and easy." At eight o'clock in the evening there were sing-songs, and later on dancing. The women who frequented those places were mostly drunken prostitutes, generally supposed to be victims of the men who employed them.

Franklin was most elaborately dressed. He had jewellery on him which must have cost many thousands of dollars. His gold watch, he said, cost nearly two hundred dollars, and would be of no more use after being so long in the water.

The mate ordered the four men down off the poop; he would not have our poop desecrated with the likes of them. The four of them came along to the galley and asked little Hughie, the cook, for a drink of hot tea, as they felt down and out after being in the water so long. We gave them some old clothes to put on until their's were dried. After sunset the wind died away, and they hailed a passing boat with the object of getting a passage on shore. When the occupants of the boat saw them they refused to give them a passage, but promised to let some of their shore friends know that they were on board.

Our steward was a man who carried a fairly good thirst

wherever he went. When he came to know that the crimps carried a bottle, he began paying attention to them and made them a good supper, and had a swig at the bottle occasionally. He invited them into his room, which was inside the saloon.

As soon as the chief mate heard them passing his door he came out and ordered them forward at once. The steward, who was now feeling " pretty good " (as the Yankees say), resented this interference on the mate's part, and asked the mate who the h——— he was, anyhow. One word led to another, and the result was the steward received a good thrashing from the mate.

When the crimps saw how the steward was manhandled they came to the conclusion that the quarter-deck was no place for them, so they came away forward to the forecastle and related what they had seen.

" I guess," said Franklin, " we shall meet that mate again before the devil meets him." The steward came along to the forecastle after he had washed himself, and we could see that he had received a fairly good trouncing.

" I guess, steward," said Franklin, " That big Bluenose mate has whaled you most unmercifully. You are looking pretty seedy, like myself. Have another drop of old Kentucky, just to show that there is no animosity between us."

" I do need a drop badly," said the steward. " I want to take action against the mate."

" Why, sure," said all four men, " we are witnesses; of course we could not interfere, as you know, but you have our sympathy. The best you can do is to take action against him, and I guess you can get a couple of thousand dollars' compensation."

The steward became quite elated over this, and could see prospects of having a good time ashore in San Francisco. He said he was none too happy on board, and would like to get out anyhow. He sneaked away aft and took a few of his belongings forward later on.

About ten o'clock a boat came alongside for the four castaways. The steward's bag was passed down into the boat, and then the steward, who had to be lowered in a bowline. We had nearly as much difficulty lowering Franklin into the boat as we had getting him on board over the taffrail.   His nerves seemed to be in a bad way; he was dead scared when we lowered him over the side.

The water was now quite smooth, and when the boat was rowed a few yards away from the ship's side the crimps commenced bawling out, "Ship ahoy!   Mister Mate, Mister Mate!" "Hallo!" answered the mate as he went up on the poop to get a better view in the darkness.

The steward now made answer, "I am going to fix you, you dirty Bluenose.   I will take action against you to-morrow.   I will make you pay through the nose.   You think you are smart; wait till you get before my lawyer."

The crimps then started on the mate : "Wait till we get you ashore," said one, "we will sandbag you and shanghai you before the mast in the hottest ship we can find, where you shall have the time of your life."

Instead of rowing ashore, the mate could see them with his night-glasses going alongside a large American ship called the W. B. Walker, which was lying close to us, and had been waiting for men for nearly a week.   This ship sailed on the afternoon of the following day, and we all came to the conclusion that the steward was packed off in her with three months' advance.   If he was put on board in place of a sailor, all we could say was "God help him," as he could never leave the deck to go aloft.   He knew nothing about sailorising in any shape or form.   The mate never received his summons to appear at court, which convinced us that the steward was taken straight from our ship to the W. B. Walker. I heard afterwards that he left about thirty-five pounds in wages behind him.

We had been lying at anchor in the bay for about six days, when the second mate returned from hospital.   I happened to be acting as steward for a few days, and was in the cabin when he came on board.

The first mate asked him how his wound was; he replied that it was quite healed up.   "And gee!" said he, "but haven't I had bad luck to get that—to get wounded, I mean.   Someone has got to sit up for this.   If I do not make sailormen claw the dust after this, I am a Dutchman!"

" You might have had worse luck," said the chief mate. " You might have been killed; mind you, the fellow was stabbing to kill."

The second mate having been off duty for quite a while, seemed unsettled and not at all inclined to go on duty again. On his second day on board the chief mate asked him what was wrong— why did he not attend to his duties?

" I guess I am going to quit," said he. " I can strike a good job on shore; in fact, it is waiting for me right now."

When the captain returned to the ship he asked to be paid off. The captain refused point-blank. " Where am I going to get another second mate?" said he. " There are no second mates here."

The second mate replied that it was the captain's business and not his to find a second mate.

One word led to another—so much so that I cleared out of the cabin in case of serious trouble arising between the two of them. How they came to settle matters I do not know. However, the second mate was paid off next day, and I suppose no one was sorry to see the last of him as he was a man-driver of the first order, but to give him credit, a smart officer and seaman.

I was relieved in the cabin by a new steward—a German about 40 years of age. He was ordered on board at eight in the morning, but did not turn up until one in the afternoon, and then so much under the influence of liquor that he went straight into his bunk. He remained there until next morning, when he came along to me to find out where all " de tings " were. I had to go round with him to show him where all the stores were, and showed him the " victualling book."

" Vat is dees," said he, " I knows noddings bout dees kind of book?"

I explained to him that all stores used were entered in the book in their proper columns, so that he could see at a glance what stores were left in the ship at any time. I pointed out each item indicated.

" Is der no gin or viskey in dees sheep?" said he.

" Not so far as I know," said I.

" Dees are a rotten sheep," said he. " I guess I quits her; dees old hooker vos no goot to me."

As the captain was on shore, I went and informed the chief mate that the new steward was not going to turn to. "All right," said he, "bring him here." He told the chief mate also that he would not turn to, and I was told to go into the cabin again. Two days afterwards another steward was shipped, a Jew, whom we afterwards called "Ikey." This man went to England in the ship. He was a very capable man and gave satisfaction to everybody.

It was about the tenth of August that we started at five in the morning to heave up the anchors, and afterwards to tow up to Port Costa, on the Sacramento River, to load a cargo of wheat bound to the Channel for orders. Campbell, the rigger, brought his men on board to assist us in unmooring and mooring at Port Costa. Campbell's men were all old sailors who had coiled up their ropes and swallowed the anchor. The morning was fine and calm, but unfortunately our steam donkey was undergoing repairs, consequently we had to heave the anchors up by hand, which made a long and tedious job.

Campbell's men were all splendid chanty men and they fairly made the harbour ring with the melody of their strong voices. The leading man was a negro who had a powerful voice. The first song was "The Banks of Sacramento." The words are :—

> "Blow, boys, blow, for Californio,
>   For there is plenty of gold,
>   So as I have been told,
>   On the banks of Sacramento," etc.

Another good chanty was :—

> "Oh, Mexico, I do very well know;
>   Hooray, Santa Anna;
>   For Santa Anna has gained the day
>   Along the plains of Mexico," etc.

Another was "Sally Brown" :—

> "Oh, Sally Brown was a bright Mulatto,
>   Was a bright Mulatto,
>   She drinks rum and chews tobacco;
>   I'll spend my money on Sally Brown," etc.

There were several fine large ships loading grain at Port Costa, which in itself was only a small village in those days. We spent about ten miserable days there, and were almost eaten up by mosquitoes at night time. They were even larger and fiercer than the Hexham greys of the Hunter River, above Newcastle, New South Wales. As no sailormen could be obtained in San Francisco to paint ship outside or bend sails, Campbell and his gang of riggers had to bend sails and paint the ship's hull before leaving Port Costa.

It was on a Sunday morning at four o'clock that we unmoored and towed down to San Francisco Bay to anchor again, and get a crew and a second mate. When we were ready for sea it so happened that very few ships were arriving, which made men scarce. Boarding houses were empty, and crimps were at their wits' end to get men. Cockney Charlie and I, being the only two men left, used to figure on the times we would have on the passage home. We had three rookies on the passage up from Australia, but on this next passage we might have a dozen or more.

The captain, apparently, had done business on former voyages with a crimp called Brennan, and one morning, when Charlie and I had rowed him ashore to the boat landing-stage, Brennan was standing at the top of the steps.

" Good morning, Brennan," said the captain, " anything doing?"

" Nop," said Brennan.

" For heaven's sake," said the captain, " can't you get me something in the shape of men. Never mind what they are; give me hobos, roughnecks, high-binders, rancheros, soldiers, priests, anything at all, so that I can get the ship out of port. What about the prison? Can't you bribe the jailers?"

" No," said Brennan. " We have done it once or twice, but you know there is such a vicious circle of preachers, rich ladies, and so forth, to take an interest in sailors now, who are commencing to shoot out their rubber necks and to poke their sticky beaks into our business, our hands are getting tied; our business is not like what it used to be."

" Cannot that vicious circle be squared somehow? "

" No," said Brennan, " those guys cannot be bought. The case is like this, cap.: the man who is prepared to give us the most blood money will be the man who will be supplied with men first. Do you get me? "

" How much blood money are you likely to demand? "

" Most likely anything from thirty to seventy dollars per man," said Brennan.

" As I have told you already, I want men," said our captain, " and you have ways and means of getting them and shanghai'ing them on board; but you are not going to get any thirty dollars out of me."

" Waal, cap.," said Brennan, " you seem to think that we keep men hanging on hooks awaiting you."

" What are you waiting for, men? " the captain demanded, turning to us.

" We are waiting for your instructions, sir," I said.

" I cannot give you any instructions at present," said the captain. " Go off to your ship."

There were three ships waiting in the bay for men besides us, and there were two ships due—one from Australia and one from Antwerp.   After we had been out in the bay about five days the vessel from Australia came in—a large four-masted vessel called the Marlborough Hill, which, being a large vessel, we expected would have a large crew.   This, however, was not the case, as she carried twelve apprentices and only seven or eight able-seamen. She was a beautiful ship and anchored not very far from us.

We could see the boats putting from the shore long before she got near the anchorage.   Those were the boarding-house runners and crimps looking for men.   We could see the mates and apprentices trying their level best to prevent them getting on board; if they were prevented in one place they would swarm on board in another part of the ship.   As the chain was rattling out through the hawse pipes, bags were going over the side into the crimps' boats, and before the ship was properly moored all her sailors were in the boats making for the water-front, all merry; we could see the bottles of old Kentucky being passed around in the boats.   By the time those men reached the water-front they would be dead drunk, and on board an outward-bound ship before morning, with three months' wages gone.

One of the three ships waiting for men was the Occidental, an American ship hailing from Bath, in the State of Maine.   This vessel had been waiting for quite a long time.   She always had a bad reputation.   Some sailormen used to say she was a floating hell with the lid off.   The men off the Marlborough Hill must have gone away in her, because she towed to sea on the following morning about eight o'clock.

AN OCEAN RACE.

A NEW second mate joined when we had been waiting in the bay for about six days, but no men. There were now four large ships at anchor waiting for crews. The new second mate was a young man, about 26 years of age, and a " towney " of the captain's from Windsor, Nova Scotia; he left a Nova Scotian vessel in Humboldt Bay and came through to join our vessel. He was a tall, well-built, and a very smart-looking man.

Day after day went, and still there were no men to be had. The boarding masters and crimps had put sailors' wages up another pound per month and demanded sixty dollars' bonus for each man put on board.

A vessel from Antwerp—a large full-rigged ship called the Andromache—came in one day at dusk and lay some distance from us; but we could not see what was going on after she anchored. On the following day two other large ships arrived—one the famous American ship, Glory of the Seas, and the other the four-masted barque Drumblair. Both vessels arrived about the same time—about five in the afternoon. They were surrounded by boats before they were well inside the Golden Gate. The Drumblair's men were seen going ashore in boats piled up high with bags and trunks, and singing :—

> " Times are hard and wages low;
> Leave her, Johnny, leave her—
> A rotten ship and a drunken crew,
> It is time for us to leave her."

It was on our eleventh day lying at anchor that the first three of our new crew came on board, and to our delight they were three Britishers who had been sailing for some few months in schooners on the Californian Coast. Their names were Tom Potter (an Englishman), James O'Neil and Tom O'Neil (from Belfast). The men were anxious to leave the coast, as the work was extremely hard, the wages too low, and the Coasting Seamen's Union had

70

burst up for want of funds. The usual three months' advance had to be paid by them to the crimps, but the O'Neil brothers had been six weeks in the boarding-house, consequently they were not much out of pocket on the whole. The three men were found to be splendid seamen, and had been shipmates before.

As a precaution, the captain had an ex-policeman engaged to watch the three men in case they deserted. It was nothing unusual for a crimp to put men on board in the morning, steal them again at night, take them to another ship, and get another sixty dollars' blood money for them. The old night watchman from the shore was paid off, and I had to go on duty in his place, along with the ex-policeman.

After everybody went to bed, the ex-policeman and I had long talks together, which made the night hours pass very quickly. He told me that he had been in the San Francisco police force for six years, and had to leave owing to getting at loggerheads with his inspector over the division of some spoils. This man said that the inspector always wanted the lion's share of every rake off, and he could not see his way clear to surrender what he considered to be his own. Shortly before he left the force he was shifted down to the water-front, where there was no end of trouble with Greeks and Japanese, and no money out of it more than his bare pay. One night three Greeks attacked him with knives. He laid the whole three out with his club, and with the assistance of another policeman he had the whole three locked up in a very short time. When giving his evidence at the court he described to the judge how the three men attacked him with knives, and how he was able to defend himself against the furious onslaught they made. The judge asked him how he managed to defend himself against three assassins. He answered: "I clubbed the sons of b———s, your worship; I guess it is a weakness I have for clubbing Greeks." The judge asked him why he did not draw his gun. He replied that he had not shot a man for the last eighteen months. The watchman informed me that he had done pretty well for himself whilst in the force; there was money everywhere to be picked up. All lawbreakers could get off if they had sufficient money to bribe the police.

On our twelfth day at anchor four more men came on board—one Swede, two negroes, and one Scotsman from Glasgow whose name was Thomson.   We were still seven men short, and the captain was getting desperate at the long delay and the extortionate amount of blood money he had to pay.

Next day boats came off every now and again with a man or two, most of whom had to be hoisted on board and dropped on the deck.   Three or four of them lay where they were dropped for some time before they were carried into the forecastle and thrown into their bunks.

Everything was got in readiness for sailing next morning, and in addition to the watchman and I keeping watch, the second mate patrolled the poop armed with a Martini rifle.   It seemed that our captain was determined to prevent any of his crew being stolen, and I presume he did not put too much trust in the ex-policeman —or in me, so far as that goes.

Next morning all hands were called at five o'clock, ready to man the windlass at half-past five.   It was my place to call all hands out, and four of the men in the forecastle were still in a dazed condition, although they had been in their bunks over thirteen hours.

One long, lanky fellow about thirty years of age asked me what kind of a bunkhouse this was, as he had never seen one like it before.   I could see that he was a cowboy or ranch hand of some kind by the clothes he had on.   I told him to get up before some of the bosses came along.   He did not seem to understand, and turned round and went to sleep again; the other three I did not bother any more about.

At half-past five I struck three bells and informed the second mate that four hands were still in their bunks.   He went along and shouted out " All hands man the windlass."   He then went into the forecastle and shook the four men up, three of whom came out on deck, but the long, lanky fellow still imagined that he was in the bunkhouse of a ranch, and would not get out.   Our last second mate would have tumbled him out on to the floor before he knew where he was, but the present second mate came away and left him lying.

We had a splendid windlass, and owing to the morning being calm we could manage easily without steam, until the anchor was up and down, or, in other words, "hove short." A very dull-looking crowd manned the capstan until Potter, the Englishman, started a chanty :—

> "We are homeward bound for Falmouth town.
> Good-bye, fare you well; good-bye, fare you well.
> Homeward bound for Falmouth town.
> Hoo-rah, my boys, we are homeward bound."

This was followed by Rio Grand :—

> "We are bound for Rio Grand,
> And away Rio, away Rio;
> Singing fare you well, my pretty young girls.
> For we are bound for Rio Grand."

The towboat came ahead and the towrope was passed on board; the anchor was hove up and we were soon towing towards the Golden Gate and leaving the city of San Francisco behind—that wicked modern Babylon. And so far as I was concerned I did not care whether I ever saw it again or not.

When we passed the Golden Gate a north-west swell came rolling up, which, with the tug pulling ahead, made us dip our hawse pipes under water—so much so that green seas were coming in through them into the forecastle. Sailors' chests, bags, boots, and clothes were washing about over the forecastle floor.

When we reached the pilot schooner the pilot left us. The wind was very light from the north. When the captain considered that we had sufficient offing, orders were given "All hands set sail." I went up to the fore topsails to loose them, and I noticed that three men were standing on the deck with a bewildered look. One was seasick and lay down on the main hatch. The second mate came along and I saw him pointing aloft to them, but they shook their heads and made for the forecastle. How times had changed with us! Had it been the last second mate they would have been laid out on the deck.

The sails were set by steam, and we were not long in piling them on to the vessel. The man who was up loosening the fore topgallant sails I could see had been at sea before, but he was a steamboat man and did not know the names of the ropes. The

F

mate was on the forecastle-head shouting out " Overhaul your leechlines," " Overhaul your buntlines and clewlines." The man had no idea what buntlines, clewlines, or leechlines meant.

We slipped the towrope as soon as the topsails, foresail and jibs were set. I remained aloft until all the sails were set on the fore, and when I came down I went into the forecastle where the chief mate was dragging the long, lanky fellow out of his bunk.

" Say, boss," said the man, " you are the first man who ever handled Long Dan in this manner, and by gosh you ain't going to tumble me out of this here bunk for nothing." At the same instant he let drive at the mate, who dodged the blow and at the same time let the man have a swinging left to the jaw. The ship was pitching and rolling, which made it impossible for a landsman to fight a seaman, and when the man saw that conditions were against him, he slunk out through the forecastle door and had to follow the crowd around the decks.

As soon as sail was set, all hands, except the man at the wheel, were sent to dinner.

After dinner all hands were called aft to answer to their names. The port forecastle door was then locked and the starboard one kept open. The chief mate and carpenter went into the forecastle, and the second mate stood at the door outside and called the men's names out. One had to pass into the forecastle at a time. Each man had to hand his sheath knife over to the carpenter, and then he had to show all his belongings in case he had brought firearms on board. After he had satisfied the chief mate he was told to walk aft to the quarterdeck and stay there until he was wanted.

All the men were examined one after the other, and only two revolvers were found amongst them—the long cowboy had one and a young hobo had one also. The cowboy seemed to be very upset when his revolver was taken from him. " I have carried that gun," said he, " for nearly five years, and now I have to part with it. I guess it is hard lines." All the sheath knives were taken along by the carpenter to his shop where he broke the points off them. They were then thrown out on deck, where every man could pick up his own knife.

At half-past five the watches were picked in the usual way. I was number one in the mate's watch, and Cockney Charlie was number one in the second mate's watch; one of the O'Neil brothers was in the mate's watch and the other in the second mate's watch. This system went on until the men were equally divided into two watches. The two O'Neils, Potter, Thomson, Davis, Rees, Cockney Charlie and I were all the Britishers in the forecastle. The other eight men were foreigners. There were two Swedes, one Frenchman, one Italian, three Americans—one of these being a negro, the other negro was a Brazilian. The Britishers were all fairly good seamen; the two Americans and the American negro had never been to sea before; the Frenchman was a steamboat sailor and was quite "green" for a while; the two Swedes were good sailormen; the Italian and the Brazilian could go aloft and follow the crowd, but on the whole were very poor sailormen.

The Liverpool ship Gaekwar was leaving San Francisco about an hour after us, also bound to Falmouth for orders. Her captain had made a bet with our captain that he would be in Falmouth before us. This vessel had the reputation of being a very fast vessel and had made a splendid passage to San Francisco. The amount of the bet was said to be twenty pounds. Each captain had implicit confidence in his ship. When we were making sail we saw the Gaekwar towing out through the Golden Gate.

During the afternoon the wind came away fresh from the north-west, and the north-west swell still increased. The yards were braced up on the starboard tack, and when I went to the wheel at four o'clock the course was "full and by." As the wind still freshened up, the yards were eased off the backstays again. The Gaekwar seemed to be gaining on us slowly, and as the wind still freshened, the order was given to clew up the royals and make them fast. The Gaekwar, which still held on to the royals, was coming up with us gradually, and by eleven o'clock was alongside us. She kept on forging ahead of us and away out to windward at the same time. At midnight nothing could be seen of her.

Orders were given about two in the morning watch to check the yards in a little more and set the royals. The wind was still strong. The log was hove after the royals were set and we were found to be doing eleven knots. At daylight we sighted the

Gaekwar on our weather beam about four miles to windward, with his royals and upper topgallant sails fast. As soon as he saw us he commenced crowding on sail again, and soon both ships were tearing along through the water about eleven knots an hour with the yards eased slightly off the backstays. The sea was now getting rough and we were throwing the spray up as high as the fore lower topsail. Both ships were carrying full sail, and not a quarter of a mile did one ship gain on the other. We could see that it would have to be a matter of strategy for one ship to gain on the other. Our captain was a hard driver, and to all appearances the captain of the other ship was the same.

At eight in the evening the weather became squally. The ships were still abreast of each other and both started to take in royals at the same time, and, after royals, upper topgallant sails. The result was that we commenced to crawl ahead of the Gaekwar. The log was hove, and we were logging as much as when we carried the royals, which went to prove that when a ship puts her lee rails into the water she is too hard pressed and will sail equally as well —if not better—when some of her upper sails are taken in. The other ship to all appearance was a much stiffer ship than ours.

The sailing ships of those days were never built to sail with a large amount of heel. When a ship heels over she commences gripping to windward, which makes it necessary to keep the helm nearly half up all the time. When a ship heels over to a great extent, the bluff of her lee bow has a tendency to throw the bow to windward, and the fuller the bows of the vessel the more she will gripe to windward.

The wind freshened up still more during the night, which made it necessary to take in lower topgallant sails, cro'jack, and mainsail. The mainsail being a large sail, it needed all hands to take it in. The three American greenhorns were seasick, and were afraid to leave the deck until they were chased off it by our new second mate. The cowboy managed to get up as far as the lower fairleads, but further he would not go. The American negro got up as high as the mainyard, and there he stuck. The other American got no further than the sheerpole.

We lost sight of the Gaekwar about nine o'clock that evening, and sighted her again at daylight next morning about five miles out on our weather quarter, with his topgallant sails set. The second mate reported this to the captain, who gave orders to set lower topgallant sails. The wind gradually eased down and all sails were set. At eight o'clock in the morning we were making ten knots, and during the forenoon the wind was aft on the starboard quarter. The Gaekwar began to overtake us gradually, and at sunset he was up alongside of us.

The three American "rookies" (as the captain called them) were brought aft and reduced to boys, their wages being only one pound per month. At this they objected and refused to work. They were then clapped in irons right away; leg-irons were put on as well as handcuffs. The cowboy showed fight, but a blow over the head with a blackjack stretched him out on the cabin floor, when he was handcuffed and leg-ironed immediately. The other two men showed no resistance. One man was put into the ship's hospital and the other two into the donkeyroom.

The captain informed them that they would get the usual food to keep their lives in—a biscuit and a cup of water daily, and as soon as they became tired of that menu and were willing to go to work, they would be released. The whole matter rested with themselves.

The cowboy was put in the hospital, as there was a prospect of the other two turning to after a couple of days' starvation. After about thirty hours in the donkeyroom the negro and the other man made up their minds to go to work, and were released right away. The cowboy, however, still refused to go to work, and persisted in this ruinous policy for nearly a whole week, when he was almost on the point of collapsing. He asked to be taken to the captain, and another man and I had to assist him along the deck and up the poop ladder. When we got him on the poop he begged the captain to let him sit on the fore cabin skylight as he was unable to stand up.

"Sit down, then," said the captain. "Look what you have brought yourself to. The whole responsibility rests on yourself; not on me. You signed an agreement to be at all times obedient to the lawful commands of your superior officers, and you refused point-blank just because I reduced your wages. You are a landsman and practically of no use to me; you are unable to go aloft to the very place where you are most needed. By your appearance and whole demeanour I take you to be a cowboy—a roughneck and a law unto yourself. You came on board here with a gun in your possession, which is against British maritime law. You signed articles to the effect that you were not to bring firearms or any offensive weapon on board, such as knuckle-dusters, slingshot, loaded cane, or bowie knife, etc., and you have deliberately broken this agreement. I wish to impress upon you that you are not on a cattle ranch now. You are on the High Seas, where I am supreme. Your opinions do not cut ice here. The crew of this ship belong to different nationalities, and every man thinks for himself and has his own opinions. It is, of course, a matter of indifference to me what any man thinks."

All the answer that the cowboy made was : " I guess the cards are stacked against me and I have got to put up with it, but I am not able to work in the condition that I am in now."

The captain gave him twenty-four hours to recuperate on, and at the end of twenty-four hours he crawled out on deck and was sent to do some odd jobs.

One of the Swedes was a man by the name of Ralph, a man about fifty-five years of age, who had sailed most of his life on British and American ships. He was a fine sailorman—steady, sober, and industrious. When he was a young man he made a voyage to San Francisco in a Swedish sailing ship, and was decoyed out of her by a man who pretended that he was a parson. Ralph was inclined to be religious. Some boarding-house runner came to know this, and invited him and another two young countrymen of his ashore to his home on a Sunday evening to have tea. The three young men were delighted with the idea, and went to the address given by the parson. After tea they became drowsy and went to sleep, and remembered nothing more until at sea on the following morning.

When Ralph awoke he found the ship pitching and rolling heavily. He went to the forecastle door, which was on the after part of the deckhouse, and on looking aloft he saw men reefing a single mizzen topsail. On looking through the forecastle he found one of his mates still asleep. They were the only two in the forecastle, and he never found out what became of the third man. He considered that they must have had a terrible dose of some abominable stuff, as they did not feel right for several days. They were on board an American ship bound for Havre, and arrived at that port when the armistice was being signed between the French and Prussians. The American ship turned out to be one of the usual kind, where the belaying pin and the blackjack were often in evidence.

The other Swede was about thirty years of age and a first-class sailorman. He had been a while in English ships, and had a great admiration for America and Americans. He tried to drawl through his nose like the Americans. We used to call him the North Sea Yank. He had acquired his American ideas when working ashore a few months in New York.

The Italian was a scatter-brained Dago, and a poor sailorman. He had a pair of old rubber boots which could not keep the water out. One night when it was cold down off the Horn, he turned in with wet feet which kept him awake for quite a while, and he became so enraged at his old boots that he jumped out of his bunk in the dark, picked up the first pair of boots that came to hand and threw them over the side. When the watch was called, Thomson, the Glasgow man, could not find his sea-boots anywhere. The Italian saw the mistake he had made right away, and offered to try and get a new pair for Thomson out of the slop-chest. He managed to get a pair for Thomson, but not for himself.

Thomson was a Glasgow rigger, supposed to be, but he was not much of a sailor, being very nervous up aloft when shortening sail or reefing a topsail in a gale of wind. Some very smart sailormen in fine weather become almost useless aloft in bad weather, and Thomson was one of these.

When a grown-up man starts going to sea—after he is twenty years of age—he can never expect to be as good a man up aloft as a man who went to sea at fifteen or sixteen years of age. When a man goes to sea at say about twenty-five years of age, everything about a sailing ship proves very irksome to him—the food, the hardships—and the dangers on deck and aloft seem too much for him.

Young boys, as a rule, have not the sense to get scared, and they become so inured to hardships and dangers aloft and on deck that they take them as they come and think nothing of it all through life. An officer trained in a steamer stands his watch on the bridge and never even gets his feet wet. Put that same officer in a sailing ship, he would leave her at the first port he touched at. He could not put up with being washed about the decks with heavy seas tumbling on board, sometimes not knowing whether he was on board or over the side.

Potter was a Lincolnshire man, and had been on the Californian Coast for some time. He came to Portland, Oregon, in an English ship from Japan, and had rather a bad experience in Portland. The crew had been a long time in that vessel. They had a considerable amount of money due them, and on arrival at Portland they requested the captain to pay them off, as they were tired of the vessel, owing to being underfed and undermanned. The captain refused to pay them off, as he would have to pay a higher wage to the next crew, and a bonus over and above that. The crimps tried their utmost to persuade them to desert, but failed to make any impression on them.

At all large American ports there are some " deadbeats " of lawyers ready to take up seamen's cases when they are having trouble with their captains or officers. One of these rascals paid the men a visit, and told them that their case against the captain was as clear as day; they had not received their proper allowance of food, and what food they received was not up to the mark, and also the ship did not carry her complement of men according to their articles of agreement; but before he could go on with the case he would need fifty dollars down. The men had no money, but said they might manage to get a few dollars apiece on Saturday evening from the captain.

When Saturday evening came they received five dollars each, which they handed over to the lawyer so that he could go ahead with the case. The lawyer came down to the ship a few days afterwards and informed them that according to the laws of the

State of Oregon that State had no jurisdiction over foreign vessels; it would therefore be necessary for them to leave the ship and take their belongings with them, declare their intentions to become American citizens, and then sue the captain of the vessel for the money due them. The men acted upon this advice and left the ship, taking their belongings with them.

The captain then made an entry in the official log that the men had deserted the ship and taken their effects with them. The fact was also reported to the British Consul. The crook lawyer could not be found as they did not even know his name. After waiting for some time they went to see the captain, who informed them that they did not belong to his ship, and that they had been absent from the ship without leave for several days—they had deserted the ship and taken their effects with them. If they had left their effects on board the circumstances would have been entirely different. The captain read the official log entry over to them. It suddenly dawned on them that they had been done in the neck by some crook who probably was not a lawyer at all.

The men then went to the British Consul and laid their case before him, who informed them that they had his sympathy, but he could not do anything for them as they were deserters in every sense of the word. They suggested that the captain bought the lawyer, but the Consul could not see his way clearly enough to believe that.

The men never received a cent of the wages due them, and the most of them had to ship in deep-water vessels again with three months' advance. Potter reckoned that he lost over thirty pounds in wages due him, and therefore made up his mind to try the coast, where the wages were better and no " dead horse " to work off.

When a sailing ship leaves a British port the crew receive one month's advance only. When that month has expired they say that the " dead horse " has been worked off, and in passenger sailing ships a horse made of straw is hoisted up and dropped over the side. After this performance the captain orders the chief steward to give the men a tot of rum each. This takes place not far from the equator when the weather is fine.

Frenchy was a man about fifty years of age and had scarcely any experience in sail except in the French Navy. He told us that he served in the French Army during the Franco-Prussian War, and spent a while as a prisoner of war in Germany. The greater part of his sea career, he said, was spent in Mediterranean steamers.

Davis was a little Cockney from Shadwell somewhere, about thirty years of age, and a foul-mouthed little rascal. He told us that he served his time on the Thames barges, held a full ticket as a London waterman, but went away deep-water when he was a little over twenty, and followed it up ever since. Although he was a small man he was a good sailorman, had plenty of grit in him, and gave one of the American rookies a good thrashing shortly after leaving San Francisco. He was, however, an out-and-out sea lawyer, and would have given no end of trouble had he been in a quiet ship.

Rees was a Welshman, about twenty-five years of age, a good seaman and a very quiet young man.

The American hobo whom Cockney Davis thrashed seemed to be about twenty-five years of age, and from his own account had never done an honest day's work in his life. He even boasted of the kind of life he had led. He said that he started when he was only fourteen years of age and had been all over the United States, a part of Canada, and also a part of Mexico. Some of his stories were rather amusing. Born in Philadelphia, he had to take to the road first of all because the police were getting to know him too well, and during all his wanderings he declared that he never got into the hands of the police again. In the spring of the year he went to Canada, and made south again during the latter part of summer. Once he crossed the Rio Grande into Mexico, but never again owing to the great dislike the Mexicans had towards the Americans. The east coast of Florida he considered to be best for winter quarters. All his long travels were by train—what he called riding the brake—jump on leaving a station and jump off just before arrival at the next station. When wandering through the farming country hobos were always guided by marks or notches under the top bar of the gate leading to the homestead. So many marks would warn them that it was a bad house, that the farmer took a gun to them, or set the dog on them. Other marks again would indicate a good house, etc. When he came on board he understood that the vessel was bound for Australia—a land of perpetual sunshine and a paradise for the hobo, where he would be called a sundowner. He considered that the American winter was too rigorous for his honourable profession.

The Brazilian negro turned out well, and was very willing to do his best. The American negro was a lazy rascal, and was turned out of the forecastle. The Brazilian was born in slavery, but was set free in accordance with some Brazilian law. That country did not liberate her slaves all at once, but by piecemeal. The first law stated that all children born after a certain date and all old people over a certain age had to be set free.

MAKING FOR THE HORN.

THE weather became very fine, and for about seven days the Gaekwar kept us company, sometimes ahead of us and sometimes as far astern. It was very difficult to say which ship was the better sailer. We were, however, of opinion that the Gaekwar was a far stiffer ship than ours and would be able to carry sail longer in a gale of wind. So far as hard driving and expert seamanship went, we could lay our captain and officers against all-comers. Our weak point, however, was the crew. We had so many useless men that no prudent captain or officer could risk carrying on hard.

Cockney Charlie always argued that in all probability the Gaekwar had as many greenhorns as we had. One thing we had in our favour was that when off the Horn we could get steam up on our donkey, and extra downhauls could be put and kept on our upper topsail yards, so that they could be hove down by steam. So far as we could see, the Gaekwar had no steam.

On our eighth day out, and about one in the morning, the wind hauled dead ahead, and the captain decided to go on the starboard tack. At daylight the Gaekwar was nowhere to be seen. He must have gone on the port tack. Our captain considered that one tack was as good as the other when the wind was dead ahead. He was also desirous of losing sight of the Gaekwar, probably so that he might be able to steal a march on him. The captain of that vessel was by all accounts a much younger man, and consequently would not be expected to have the same experience as our captain.

We kept on the starboard tack about thirty-six hours or thereabout, when the wind drawing more ahead it became necessary to tack ship. The average time taken to tack a ship of our size and build in a good working breeze is twenty minutes, but having so many deadheads, this time it took twenty-seven minutes. Time counts from the time the captain calls out " Helm's a lee " until the time everything is set on the other tack. There is some

84

excitement when tacking a large sailing ship. The officers are bawling out orders and the crew hey-hoing on the ropes. Every man must know his own particular station.

The first order is : " All hands tack ship." The next order : " Haul the cro'jack and mainsail up "; then " Down main topmast staysail." Next order is : " Stations." The captain is on the poop and orders the man at the wheel to put his helm down gradually. The ship comes up, and the captain calls out from the front of the poop " Helm's a lee." Fore and head sheets are then eased off, and the ship comes up in the wind. The captain then must judge the proper time when to swing the main and cro'jack yards, when he gives the order " Mainsail haul." When properly judged the afteryards will swing round to the backstays faster than the crew can gather in the slack. When the afteryards are braced right up, the next order is : " Fore bowline, let go and haul," and round comes the foreyards, but very slowly until the weather clew of the foresail begins to fill. Very few ships are well enough manned to work the mainsail; they generally haul it up instead. It is the usual thing for the captain to call out " Mainsail haul," but by rights it should be " Main topsail haul " when the mainsail is hauled up.

We did not get north-east trades until our tenth day out, when they came away quite fresh; yards were squared and we made a good eight knots. There was still no sight of the Gaekwar, but we all came to the conclusion that she was well to the westward of us. As soon as the captain made sure that we had the north-east trades we started shifting sails. The number one, or hard-weather suit was bent leaving 'Frisco, but the fine-weather suit had to be bent now, and kept up until we got to the southern edge of the south-east trades.

On the passage from Newcastle, New South Wales, to Fort San Diego we got no afternoon watch below, but after leaving the latter port for San Francisco we got our afternoon watch below, as we found that the chief mate was dead against keeping us up. Although the chief mate was a hard man, he believed in giving every man a fair deal. He was as honest as the day, but he expected his pound of flesh. He was very severe on any man whom he found loafing or malingering, but if he found a man actually sick he was as gentle as a woman. This hard-looking, taciturn man surprised us when he used to dress the men's salt water boils down off the Horn.

The second mate who left in San Francisco was really an evil genius on board, and after he left the ship everything was entirely different; there was no bullying and kicking of men who could not retaliate.

The captain, beyond doubt, had been a bully when the last second mate was with us. After he left, when he knocked the long cowboy down with a blackjack, that was the only bullying we saw him do. Although he used to swear hard at men afterwards, he never lifted his hand.

The new second mate turned out to be a very smart officer and seaman. Although he made every man understand that he was an officer, and they were the men before the mast, he never got throwing out his chest, as the Americans say. He was as hard as nails, like a cat aloft. He was, like Cockney Charlie, " a child of the sea." He was, of course, a Bluenose (Nova Scotian), ever ready with his fist or belaying pin when a man became insolent towards him. I met him eleven years afterwards (1896) in Rio de Janeiro. I was then in command of a fine clipper ship which had been a passenger ship to Australia, and he was in command of a large Liverpool four-masted barque.

Three of us left Rio de Janeiro for New York in ballast on the same day. He left about an hour before me and I arrived in New York twelve days ahead of him, and sixteen days ahead of the other ship. Ballast was expensive in Rio; both ships were modern and needed more ballast than they took in. My ship was of the clipper type, well ballasted, and could fetch where she looked, and was not a hard-mouthed ship.

We had fine weather all through the north-east trades and very little doldrums around the equator. We crossed the equator on our twenty-third day out, and Cockney Charlie, the O'Neil brothers, Potter, and all the rest of us Britishers, asked permission to celebrate the event and bring Neptune on board.

The celebration took place on a Saturday evening about six

o'clock. Tom O'Neil was dressed up as Neptune, James O'Neil and I were the policemen, Cockney Charlie the doctor, and Potter the barber. Neptune was dressed as a king with long flowing beard made out of manilla rope, a tin crown on his head, and a trident in his hand. We all marched aft on the quarter-deck and asked to see the captain. Neptune handed the captain an illuminated address, which had been read out to him previously.

The captain took the whole proceeding in good part, and when Neptune remarked that we would first sample his rum, and then we would proceed to administer justice to those men who had trespassed on his domains for the first time, the steward was ordered to give us all a tot of rum; we all drank his health and went about our business. A large wash-deck tub stood on the deck full of water, a forecastle seat was set up against it. Neptune sat on his throne close by in his regal robes, with trident in hand. James O'Neil and I were ordered to bring the trespassers along to get sentence passed on them, and then to get shaved by the barber. The barber's razor-blade was a half-inch board about fifteen inches long and three inches wide, with an edge on it. The lather was composed of soft soap, water and soot. The shaving brush was the end cut off a five-inch manila hauling line, the brush part being long and swabby.

The first man we brought along was the long cowboy, who offered no resistance as each of us had a baton in our hands. He was made to stand before Neptune, who reprimanded him for trespassing on Neptune's domains, and sentenced him to be shaved and washed. He was then set on the bench with his back to the tub, each policeman holding him. The barber then started laying on the lather, and brought his wooden razor on to his face. He was then tumbled backwards into the tub of water and his head kept under water for a few seconds.

The other young Yankee crawled up aloft to the futtock shrouds, and remained there. We two policemen went up after him, and when he refused to go down we decided to use force; we tied a rope round him and lowered him down. Needless to say, he received an extra good shave and a longer time under the water than any of the others.

The south-east trades came along about a degree south of the line. The wind was very light when a heavy bank set up in the south-east and gradually spread over the whole horizon in that direction. The chief mate was on duty, the time being about ten p.m. We were all sitting on the main hatch when the chief mate shouted out : " Brail in the spanker "; then " Haul the cro'jack up "; then " Haul the mainsail up." All hands in the watch were standing by when down the squall came. " Stand by royal halyards," shouted the mate; " Lower away royal halyards "; and next " Square the cro'jack yard." We were struck flat aback and lay over to an angle of fifteen degrees. The squall soon passed over; yards were trimmed, royals set, and we were soon going through the water about eight knots.

We had the south-east trades all right, which were quite fresh at times. All hands of the watch on deck were now kept busy cleaning bright work. This means cleaning the varnish off the teak-wood with sand and canvas. The rigging had been rattled down before reaching the equator. This is considered a very particular job, and only the best sailormen are sent to it. A good sailorman is supposed to put on eight ratlines in the lower rigging in a watch. The poorer type of sailorman is sent to the topmast and topgallant rigging.

When the cleaning of bright work was stopped, we started tarring down the rigging, which is considered a very particular job. Frenchy was sent to tar down on the mizzen mast. He had to climb up the royal backstays to the royal masthead and work down. He was sent to this mast as he would only have a short distance to climb. When he got to the topgallant masthead he started shinning up the royal backstay; the lanyard of the tar-pot carried away and down it came, striking the outrigger on its way down. The tar came down like a shower-bath all over the sails, mast, poop, and captain. The captain fairly roared at Frenchy, called him all the useless, good-for-nothing, frog-eating hobos of a Frenchman. When Frenchy came down he was also in a mess, and his nerves were completely upset; probably he was afraid of getting a beating.

We started to get our hard-weather clothes ready for Cape Horn shortly after crossing the equator. All of us who had oilskins started oiling them so that they would be dry before getting down south. The three hobos had no oilskins or seaboots, and some of the other men had old oilskins and old seaboots which most probably would be done before reaching the Horn. Our oilskins were oiled with boiled linseed oil, as the chief mate could not spare us raw oil. Time was short in any case, and boiled oil dries quicker. The oilskins receive a light coat of oil; the coats are hung up in the sun, the sleeves being extended with a broom handle through them, and the pants are sort of inflated on a barrel hoop.

Every sailorman was busy making preparations of some sort. Frenchy was lining his overcoat with an old blanket; this coat was for the wheel and look-out. He had no seaboots, but was hoping that the captain would let him have a pair out of the slop-chest. We all told him that he might as well look for last year's snow as look for a pair of boots from the captain for the next few months at anyrate, seeing that he had three months' advance. Little Cockney Davis from Shadwell needed boots badly also, but he was expecting that Rees, the Welshman, would lend his pair, seeing that they were in different watches.

We had splendid weather all through the south-east trades, the ship averaging sometimes as much as eight knots. We started shifting our sails in about twenty degrees south when we were losing the south-east trades. The wind was light and the weather fine, which enabled us to shift all the sails in one day, which was very good considering how badly we were manned. In the tropics the second suit of sails is used, but outside of the tropics the very best suit must be carried.

It was on a fine Sunday morning that we sighted Pitcairn Island about ten miles distant. Owing to the direction of the wind we could not pass closer to it than seven miles. This island is in latitude 25 south and longitude 130 west. Ships from 'Frisco bound round Cape Horn generally sight this island, and pass close to it so that the natives can come off in their boats with fruit and vegetables to exchange for clothing, chinaware, tobacco, etc.

The inhabitants of the island are descendants of the mutineers of H.M.S. Bounty, who settled there after the mutiny. The

G

Bounty was commanded by Captain Bligh, who was one of the worst tyrants that ever commanded a ship. To give him credit, he was a man of great courage and resource, for, after he and his officers were cast into the ship's boats by the mutineers, they covered thousands of miles in those open boats and finally reached England. This was in 1787. It was never known what became of the Bounty until nearly forty years afterwards, when a passing ship visited the island. All the mutineers were then dead except one man, by the name of Adams, who reigned over it as a sort of patriarch.

Twenty years after the mutiny, when Bligh was an admiral, he was appointed Governor of New South Wales. He was still a tyrant. He even quarrelled with the officers of the ship on his way out to Australia. He had not been many weeks in Australia when his tyrannical temper got the better of him, which ended up in a revolution headed by a Captain MacArthur, who had been an officer in a New South Wales regiment. The revolution ended in Bligh being made a prisoner by the insurgents, and another man acted in his place until a Governor was sent out from England.

After the mutiny on the Bounty the mutineers visited the Society Islands, and taking wives with them set sail again for Pitcairn Island.

About two or three days after passing Pitcairn Island the wind came away fresh from the north-west, and we sighted a vessel early in the morning. At about three in the afternoon we were up alongside of her. She was the Earnock, of Belfast, whose captain informed us that the Gaekwar passed him about daybreak that morning. The wind was now blowing fresh on our starboard quarter, and we were doing about nine knots, with all sail set.

On receiving this news all hands were more or less excited, and there was an extra sweating up on sheets and halyards, so that everything could draw to the best advantage. We sighted the Gaekwar early on the following morning about five miles ahead of us. The wind was now strong from the westward and both ships were still swinging under full sail and doing about fourteen knots. As before, neither ship seemed to gain on the other. The weather became colder every day, especially after getting down into the roaring forties. A deputation went aft to see the captain about getting some more food as the weather was getting colder, and after some discussion he agreed to give us burgoo and molasses one morning and mush on the following morning whilst we were in cold weather. Burgoo is the sailor's name for oatmeal porridge, and mush is ground maize, generally called Indian meal.

A very heavy squall struck us in about 49 south, which carried away our mizzen royal brace and the weather sheet. The jerk was so sudden and heavy that the yard broke in two. The fore and main royals were taken in, in case a like catastrophe happened to them. The accident occurred just before dusk, and we had a high old time aloft that night sending the wreckage down. The night was pitch dark and the ship rolling rails under on each side. It was just the kind of night to try any man's mettle. The broken-off part of the yard would swing away out from the ship and come back against the mast and rigging with such force as to break everything it came up against. The crossjack was torn badly, through the broken end of the spar piercing the canvas.

The captain and the chief mate had a row over this business. The captain contended that the wire brace runner was too old and should have been replaced. The chief mate reminded the captain that he had asked for wire in San Francisco and never got it. There was, by all accounts, some very plain speaking on both sides over this mizzen royal brace. This was the first time we knew of any friction between the captain and chief mate, and of course our sympathies were entirely with the latter, as the royals should have been taken in long before. It took about four hours to send the wreckage down and furl the crossjack, which had to be repaired up aloft where it was.

At two o'clock in the morning, as the wind came away strong from the south-west, with a high sea running, all hands were called out to shorten sail. The night was still pitch-dark and the decks were full up the whole time, which made it almost impossible for the men to haul on the ropes.

After being called out to shorten sail, the first order was, " Haul the mainsail up, man weather gear." Several times we were washed away by the heavy seas tumbling on board. One sea smashed the starboard lifeboat to pieces, all of which went over the side with the next sea. The mainsail was eventually hauled up without anyone getting seriously hurt by the huge greybeards which were tumbling on board. The sail bellied out like a balloon away above our heads, threatening every time it flapped to knock us off the yard. The contest was a severe one; it was a battle between a handful of men and a huge sail ninety-two feet in breadth and forty-six feet deep. All hands, including the carpenter, sailmaker, and three hobos, were aloft on the yard. Sometimes we would have a part of the sail spilled, when a stronger gust of wind would blow it out of our hands before anyone could get a turn of a gasket around it.

The language on that yard was full of sulphur, and although the weather was bitterly cold, every man was sweating, wet clothes and all on. The three hobos, of course, were no use to us, but only in the way. The second mate, who was on the middle of the yard, ordered them away. It took nearly two and a half hours to get the sail in.

The six topgallant sails and two jibs were the next to be taken in, which, being small sails, was easily done. The wind was now, at daylight, right abeam. We were logging fourteen knots, under six topsails and foresail, and towering seas were tumbling on board all over the main deck, and the lee sheerpoles went under with the lee rolls.

Davis, the little Cockney from Shadwell, was sent away from the wheel by the chief mate for giving insolence during the time we were shortening sail. This man, if he is still alive, should make a splendid trade union agitator. He seemed to look for trouble, and every time during the night that we were called along to trim yards, set, or take in sail, he would start grumbling, and would remark that all those jobs were not necessary, and were really worked-up jobs to keep us on the move.

The south-west gale eased up in the evening and all sail was set again, except the mizzen royal as the yard was broken. A new yard was made after we rounded the Horn.

The weather was now getting cold, and most of the men were very badly off for clothing, seaboots and oilskins. Some had not even the donkey's breakfast or blankets. We all knew that the captain had all these necessaries in the slop-chest, and several of the men went to him and begged him to let them have some clothes. He, however, refused point-blank to supply them with anything until the " dead horse " was worked up, which would be three months after leaving San Francisco. Tobacco was only served out once a month, a pound at a time, except in the case of Cockney Charlie and I, who were served with as much tobacco as we wanted.

Some of the men could smoke and chew a pound of tobacco in two weeks, and when their allowance was done they started to play poker in an endeavour to replenish their slender supplies. They generally started when they had a two-ounce plug left, and often with good success. Larsen, the Swede, was one of the heavy smokers, an expert player at poker, and sometimes had five or six pounds in his possession after an hour's play. Matches also became scarce, which made it necessary for the men to keep a lamp burning in the forecastle day and night. When the captain was informed by someone that an enormous amount of oil was being used in the forecastle, we were put on an allowance of one pint a week. Sailormen are very resourceful men and were not to be beaten for want of light; consequently several slush lamps were made. This is done by putting galley slush into a tin, and using a strip of canvas for a wick. The wick is held in position by a piece of thin wire stretched across the tin.

The weather remained very fine for about four days after the last blow, but when we got down into the fifties the weather became very cold and squally. Some of the squalls were exceptionally heavy.

A large amount of our coal cargo had been passed into the forepeak on the passage from Fort San Diego to 'Frisco; this now came in handy down off the Horn for keeping steam on the donkey boiler, and for drying our clothes. Had it not been for this fire, several of the men would have died through having to put wet clothes on.

A VERY "WET" SHIP.

ONE storm after another was experienced when we reached the roaring forties; decks were swept fore and aft by heavy seas tumbling on board. The wind was westerly nearly all the time after passing the fiftieth parallel of latitude : men would scarcely be warm in bed before they were called out again to shorten sail; and a few hours afterwards the sails would be set again. Sometimes the sails would be split in the setting owing to the wind being so strong. The captain scarcely ever went below, but was either on the poop or in the chart house, where his food was brought up to him.

Some of our men were terribly fatigued, though those of us who were young did not mind the severe ordeal we were passing through. We were getting quite used to being washed by the heavy seas from one end of the ship to the other. Our clothes were never dry when we were on deck. When we went below, we would change and take the wet clothes to the donkeyroom to dry, ready to put on again when we were called. Two men were at the wheel constantly for three days.

The weather became bitterly cold when we reached the latitude of Cape Horn—sleet, snow or hail squalls at very short intervals. The snow squalls were blinding; we could not see a ship's length ahead, and still we went tearing along wildly, sometimes making as much as fourteen knots an hour.

The two men at the wheel toiled like Spartans, and although the weather was bitterly cold, they were wet with perspiration. The ship was so hardly pressed that she would sheer a couple of points to each side of her course. During one of those sheers a heavy dollop came over that smashed in the starboard galley door, sending pots and pans floating over the galley floor. One enormous sea which came in over the starboard side amidships bashed in the door of the carpenter's room. The water was knee-deep for a few minutes in the forecastle, although it was a topgallant forecastle. We often cursed the Gaekwar, as being the cause of all this hard driving. The ship was too hard pressed, although, beyond doubt, she was a very wet ship.

As we were getting well down towards the Horn by dead reckoning, the captain became very anxious about his position. Dead reckoning at its best is very unreliable, as it is hard to tell what sort of a course the ship makes when she steers so badly.

We all had a pretty good idea that we were getting near the Horn. The carpenter had been engaged doing something in the mate's room, and the log book, newly written up, lying open on the mate's desk, the carpenter seized the opportunity of noting the position and brought it to me. From the position given me, I made the Diego Ramirez Islands to bear S. 86 E. 201 miles, which, at the speed we were doing, should be sighted at five o'clock next morning. This course and distance being only by dead reckoning might be twenty or thirty miles out, or even more.

At ten o'clock that night, when another man and I were being relieved at the wheel, we overheard the chief mate say to the captain that it was sheer madness to drag on sail much longer. The wind was still strong and the weather thick, and we were liable to run into an outward bound ship at any minute.

About half past ten we heard the long-awaited order, " Mizzen lower topsail down hauls, two hands take in the slack of the lee brace." After this sail was furled and hands down from aloft, the next order was, " Main topgallant down hauls." The main lower topgallant sail was clewed up, and both sails made fast at the same time. At midnight all hands took in the mizzen lower topsail, and fore and main upper topsails. After those sails were furled, the ship went along beautifully under two lower topsails, reefed foresail, and fore topmast staysail.

It was the spring of the year down off the Horn and consequently the days were getting long. About one o'clock next morning the wind fell away light and backed to the north-west, which is a very bad sign in those high southern latitudes. The sea was still heavy, and the ship was rolling it in over one side and out over the other side. At daylight the weather was clear enough to see three or four miles ahead, and the wind being light, more sail had to be set.

About six o'clock in the morning when Rees, the Welshman, was up aloft loosing the fore lower topgallant sail, he sighted land about two points on the starboard bow. The captain was on the poop at the time, and shouted to the second mate to go up on the fore and see what the fool of a man reckoned he saw.

As soon as the second mate got up as high as the fore yard, he shouted out, " Hard aport ; the land is only about two or three miles off."

" All hands on deck at once," the captain bawled out. " Never mind clothes, come as you are, we are nearly on the rocks."

In less than a minute all hands were at the braces, and the ship was braced up on the starboard tack so that we weathered the rocks about half a mile. The captain was not sure whether the rocks were the Diego Ramirez Islands, or the Iledefonso Islands away further north. If the latter, it was necessary to weather them. As soon as we weathered them he identified them as being the Diego Ramirez, which we could have passed to the northward. The weather was still thick away to the eastward, but as the captain was now sure of his position he gave orders to pile on the sail.

The ship evidently was nearly forty miles ahead of dead reckoning. All sail was set except the mainsail and crossjack. The wind was fresh from the north-west, and we were bowling along at about ten knots, when we went nearly on the top of a large American ship outward bound. This vessel was also being driven for all she was worth, under six topsails and foresail, but was making far better weather of it than we were doing, although we were running free. We were so close to her before we saw her that we only cleared her about six hundred feet. We could hear the officer on her poop swearing at us.

We passed the eastern end of Staten Island in the afternoon. A more desolate-looking place could not be seen anywhere. Everyone on board was glad to get round the Horn so easily ; every day should bring us into finer weather. About midnight, when we were careering along with all sail set, a terrific squall came away from the north-west, with hail and a biting cold. All hands had to shorten sail again, which took us until daylight, when the wind chopped suddenly into the south-west and blew fiercer than ever. Hailstones came down as large as marbles, and after that sometimes sleet and sometimes snow.

This south-west gale still increased in force; a tremendous sea got up and avalanches of water tumbled on board continuously. Frenchy and Thomson were at the wheel, and had to be relieved, as both men became dead scared of being washed away. The men became nervous, and were always looking over their shoulders at the greybeards coming up from behind. We were still running under a heavy press of sail—six topsails, full foresail and main lower topgallant sail. Frenchy and Thomson were relieved at the wheel by James O'Neil and Potter, both splendid helmsmen.

Terrific seas were now running, and we could scarcely see a ship's length ahead during the snow squalls; the decks were full up the whole time, sometimes only the tops of the houses in sight. The captain and second mate both stood near the wheel watching the steering, but still no word of shortening sail. During the heavy squalls the night was as dark as pitch; still the brave ship struggled along like a thoroughbred. Everyone of us came to the conclusion that the captain was either mad through want of sleep or else drunk.

Ralph Wiberg, the most experienced man in the forecastle, took it upon himself to go and call the chief mate and explain to him what like the weather was. The chief mate was up on the poop in a few minutes. What passed between the captain and mate we never knew. The order came from the poop a few minutes afterwards, " All hands shorten sail; the watch on deck see main lower topgallant gear all clear." As soon as all hands reached the deck and manned the gear the weather sheet was slacked away; a big sea tumbled on top of us and washed us all over the deck. The sail gave one terrific flap and went into pieces.

The next was the mizzen upper topsail, which was taken in after a great struggle, and then the fore upper topsail, which was taken in easily, as the ship was scudding before the wind and this topsail was becalmed by the main. The foresail was the next to be taken in. The foreyards were braced up so that the flat of the sail was not exposed to the wind. After this sail was made fast, the foreyards were squared in again as before. The wind and sea were still increasing, and it was snowing continuously, but as luck would have it we had daylight after the foresail was furled.

At four o'clock in the morning it was Rees's and Davis's turn at the wheel, and about half past five we pooped a tremendous sea which washed the two men away from the wheel and down on the main deck. Strange to relate, they were not very much hurt. Davis made straight for the forecastle, whilst Rees, the Welshman, managed to get on the fore-and-aft bridge and made a dash for the wheel, which was spinning around. The chief mate, who was conning the helmsmen at the time the sea came over, was washed off the poop also. He picked himself up on the main deck and made for the poop as fast as he could, although his right shoulder was out of joint.

The captain and the Welshman were the first to grab the wheel, but they were too late. The ship broached-to, went nearly on her beam ends, and became completely unmanageable. She went over so far sometimes that the lower yards almost touched the water. Broaching-to when running before a heavy gale has been responsible for the loss of many a fine ship.

Although the grain cargo was well secured against shifting, some of the men were afraid that the shifting boards would carry away and the cargo go over to leeward and thus capsize the ship. As soon as circumstances permitted, the second mate went below into the hold, and reported everything all right down there.

As the fore braces led on to the forecastle head, which was then the driest part of the ship, the foreyards were braced up far enough to fill on the fore lower topsail, and fore topmast staysail was set so as to pay the vessel's head off and get her once more before the wind and sea. During this operation the chief mate sent me below to the lamp-room to fill a gunny bag partly up with oakum and then pour a couple of gallons of pine oil into it, and throw it over the weather side with a rope attached to it. Whilst I was in the lamp-room a tremendous sea tumbled on board, sweeping the ship fore and aft. She quivered all over, and went over almost on her beam ends. I heard the mate bawl out, " Belay and hang on for your lives." I fully expected that every man would have been washed overboard, or perhaps some of them be floating about in the water with broken limbs. Fortunately, all of them managed to hang on, and no one was hurt.

I made a rush for the weather fore rigging and threw the bag of oil over the weather side, slacking away rope until it was away about fifty or sixty feet to windward. The effect of the oil on the water was marvellous : the waves were still as mountainous as before, but did not break. I looked over to leeward from my position in the fore rigging, and saw that the whole of the lee bulwarks were gone, all boats were gone, the two large spars for spare topmasts had broken loose and were floating about the deck threatening to knock everything to pieces that came in their way.

The ship was eventually got before the wind again, and ran for the next six or seven hours under two lower topsails. Two men were kept at the wheel with lashings round them. Wiberg and I were both at the wheel together, and would have been washed away several times if we had not been securely lashed. The weather was still bitterly cold, but clear ahead except during the hail squalls, which sometimes lasted for half an hour. Although the weather was cold we were sweating at the wheel owing to the seas throwing the ship about, sometimes as much as three points on either side of her course. Sails were set again as soon as the weather moderated, and soon we were bowling along at 10 knots before a fresh south-wester, which unfortunately fell away light and backed to the north-west.

It was on a fine Sunday forenoon when we sighted five large icebergs, ranging from 200 to 500 feet high. The captain decided to go in between the two largest ones, which were nearly a mile apart. The weather was exceptionally fine for that part of the world. The wind was still north-west, the sea was smooth, with a slight south-west swell running, and our position was somewhere about 180 miles north-east of the Falkland Islands. A man was stationed on the forecastle-head to report if the ship was likely to hit any small pieces of ice which came in our way.

The wind remained very light all afternoon. We would have

averaged about five knots or thereabout, and we were still meeting in with bergs of all sizes, some of which were only a few feet high. About six o'clock in the evening they were thicker than ever; it was " Hard up " the helm, or " Hard down " the whole time, so as to avoid the small bergs.   At sunset the captain became very anxious, and sent the second mate aloft to scan the horizon and find out the easiest way of clearing the icebergs.   We were at that time abreast of a berg about ten or twelve miles long, about fifty feet high, and flat on the top.   The second mate reported a fairly large opening about two points on the starboard bow.   The ship was kept away for this opening, which must have been about twenty miles distant, as it was nearly midnight before we got there.

More icebergs showed up—there seemed to be no end to them— and about two or three o'clock in the morning the weather became thick, and we found ourselves up alongside a huge one about 200 feet high.   All hands had been standing by all night, ready for a call to the braces.   We were only about half a mile away when a huge mass was sighted from right ahead to two points on the port bow.   Helm was immediately put hard up, and orders were given to haul mainsail up and square afteryards.   The next order was, " Stand by to square foreyards."   In wearing round we cleared the berg by about a ship's length only, and ran up against a small berg about forty feet high and shaped like a minaret, the whole top of which tumbled down on our deck alongside the main hatch and bent the deck beams down about six inches.   The captain estimated that the weight of ice landed on our deck was over thirty tons.   Orders were given for the carpenter to sound the pump well, which was found to be quite dry.

Daylight came about an hour afterwards, and as the morning brightened up we could see icebergs all round us—large and small. The captain decided to go more to the eastward, as there would be more chance of getting clear of the icebergs.   The course was therefore altered three points more to the eastward, and at five o'clock in the evening we passed about ten miles to the eastward of the last of them.   The weather still kept fine and no more bergs were seen.

Icebergs come from that great storehouse of ice in the

Antarctic regions away south-west of Cape Horn, and drift to the north-eastward in the Antarctic drift current, helped by the south-west gales. After following a north-east course as far as about 200 miles north-east of the Falkland Islands, they follow an easterly track across the South Atlantic and pass the Cape of Good Hope at a distance of 300 to 400 miles to the southward. In very heavy weather pieces break off those huge bergs. It is nothing unusual to see pieces breaking off weighing two or three hundred tons, which make a terrific noise as they fall into the water. That is called " calving."

For about three weeks the strain on the crew had been terrific. Nearly everyone had saltwater boils, caused by the long exposure to salt water and cold weather. The cowboy and the other American hobos were laid up through saltwater boils and frost-bitten toes. The Italian and the Frenchman were both used up and unfit to do any work : their nerves were completely shattered, and they had rheumatism. The chief mate and steward had to spend a while each day doctoring the sick.

During the gale the heavy seas had played havoc around the deck ; in addition to the bulwarks being gone all along one side, nearly every door had been smashed in. The galley had been gutted out ; the galley range was broken to pieces, so that it was of no more use for cooking purposes. Salt water had got into the storeroom and damaged most of the provisions. Tea, coffee, and sugar were all completely spoiled. The water had also found its way from the storeroom down to the cargo. The mainyard was badly bent through coming into contact with the iceberg ; one of its truss-pins was broken.

Although the ship's hull ground against the iceberg she made no water. About a week after we collided with the iceberg the chief mate discovered a fracture in the rudder-head, which must have been done when the men were washed away from the wheel and the rudder took charge. As soon as the captain saw this he decided to shape a course for Monte Video, and if he could not make that port to try and make Rio de Janeiro.

We all hoped the wind would keep out of the west, so that we could make Monte Video and avoid Rio, owing to the yellow fever season being on. The wind did keep favourable, and we anchored off the town of Monte Video on a fine Sunday morning. Fresh provisions were brought off in time for our tea, and we all had a royal time.   Sometime during the night the three hobos, Frenchy, and the Italian deserted.   Harry the Greek, a well-known boarding-house keeper, sent his runner off shortly after we anchored, when arrangements must have been made with the deserters for his return later on.   We were all glad to see the last of those five men, as they were of little use on board any ship.

Five days passed before repairs were started, and then a gang of men commenced on the bulwarks and rudder-head.   The delay in starting would be owing to the captain awaiting his owner's instructions, holding surveys, calling tenders, etc.

The town of Monte Video does not have an imposing appearance as seen from the anchorage, although there are some very fine buildings in it.   The streets are badly paved, having large ruts here and there, and the tramways are drawn by mules.   The port of Monte Video is easily made, and is handy for damaged ships putting into for repairs.   Many ships have had to put into this port for repairs after beating off Cape Horn for weeks.   One coal laden ship was there with her cargo heated; she had been beating off the Horn for a long time and then turned round and made for Monte Video.

Coal laden ships of those days had sounding pipes in their holds to carry the foul air up from below, and also for lowering a thermometer to ascertain whether the coal was becoming heated or not.   When the vessel mentioned arrived in Monte Video, arrangements were made to hold a survey on the following day, and shortly before the hour arranged for this, the ship's carpenter went and dropped hot rivets down the sounding pipes so that the thermometer would show a high temperature at the time of survey.   The surveyors would then make out their reports and recommend that the cargo be discharged so as to reach the seat of the fire.   It happened very often that the whole cargo was left in Monte Video, owing to its being considered a dangerous kind of coal and not fit to be long in a ship's hold.

Our repairs were completed in sixteen days, which was considered quite a record for Monte Video at that time. The damaged grain was brought up on deck and dried in the sun, and afterwards put into the hold again. The captain purchased two lifeboats and a dinghy which had formerly belonged to a vessel which had been condemned there as a constructive total loss.

Five new men were shipped in the places of those who deserted; three of them were Britishers and the other two were Swedes. They all had a month's advance, and they turned out to be good sailormen. We had been twenty-two days in Monte Video when we set sail early on a Monday morning with a fine westerly breeze.

The three Britishers who were shipped at Monte Video were, Flood, an Irishman; Bob, a Cockney from Poplar; and Geordie, from Shields. Flood and Geordie were men under thirty, and Bob, the Cockney, would be somewhere about forty-five.

It was a strange coincidence that Ralph Wiberg the Swede and Bob the Cockney had both been shipmates many years before, and were not aware of it until Ralph was relating an incident which happened on Green's Carlisle Castle about ten years before that. By comparing notes, they found that they were both together on that particular voyage.

Ralph Wiberg had spent many years in the Australian passenger ships. He made a round voyage in the Marco Polo when Bully Forbes commanded that vessel. Bully Forbes was the same man who commanded the Lightning when Billy Barton was mate. Although Billy Barton and Ralph never met, their descriptions of Bully Forbes were very similar, although one was an officer with Forbes and the other a man before the mast.

Bully Forbes's proper name was James Nicol Forbes, a native of Aberdeen, who went to sea a poor boy and rose to the command of two of the finest ships afloat at that particular time. Bully Forbes was the Napoleon of the Mercantile Marine, and, like the Little Corporal, he rose like a rocket. The passages he made were astounding. He beat some fast ships when he was in command of old wooden tubs that could scarcely get out of their own way with other men.

He was a man who did not know what fear meant, and was a seaman and navigator second to none. He was vain and boastful, through being so much fêted by his employers and shipping people in Liverpool and in Australia, and he became as proud as a Spanish Grandee.   When he was appointed to command the fine new ship Schomberg, a banquet was given in his honour by the Liverpool shipowners and merchants a day or two prior to his sailing from that port.   At this banquet he made a very bombastic and silly speech, and finished it off by saying, " It is hell or Melbourne Heads in sixty days.   I am going to make a passage this time that will astonish God Almighty."   Some say that the astonishing of the Almighty was left out of it.   Be that as it may, he piled the Schomberg up near Curdie's Inlet—not far from Moonlight Head on the Victorian Coast—on her sixtieth day out.   After that he was a broken man and sank into obscurity.   Success has turned many a sea captain's head as well as Bully Forbes's.

THE GAEKWAR AGAIN.

OUR second suit of sails was bent before leaving Monte Video, and we started holystoning the decks shortly after leaving. The deck is wet first, and sand sprinkled over it. The men then have to get down on their knees and rub the deck with a piece of sandstone until the wood is white.

The south-east trade winds came away fresh, and in a few days we were across the equator. There we lost the trade winds and found ourselves in a calm belt. This calm belt is called the doldrums; the rain falls in torrents, and sometimes a puff of wind comes from one direction and then a puff from another. Every advantage must be taken of every little puff so as to get the ship across this calm belt. It is murderous work hauling the yards around almost continuously, either under a broiling hot sun or else with the rain falling in torrents. The weather being hot, no man can stand oilskins during these torrential rains, which sometimes last for several hours.

Every man takes advantage of equatorial rains, as this is the only time he can get water to wash his clothes. According to the Board of Trade scale a seaman can only claim three quarts of water per day, and the greater part of that amount has to go to the galley for cooking purposes. Sailing ships built in the late eighties were supplied with tanks sufficient to hold six months' water, and could afford to give each man a gallon per day. Some ships were supplied with condensers or distilling machinery, which often came in useful.

We crossed the equator further west than is usually done, and sighted St. Paul Rocks, about five or six miles to the westward, at daybreak one morning. We were becalmed at the time, and we could see that the current was setting us straight towards them. Orders were given to have two boats ready for swinging out in case they were needed to tow the ship a couple of miles further ahead to enable us to drift clear of the rocks.

105

Davis, the Cockney, remained in the forecastle, smoking, whilst the rest of us were getting the boats ready. The chief mate missing him, went to the forecastle door and asked him why he was not on deck like all the other men. Davis took the old clay pipe out of his mouth and threw it at the chief mate, shouting, " You bleeding ———— of a blue-nose, I have had enough of you." The mate rushed into the forecastle at once and dragged the Cockney out on deck. Cockney was a small man in comparison to the mate; he tried to put up a good fight, but was no match for his opponent, who was a very powerful and active man. The first blow stretched poor Cockney out on the deck. He rose looking groggy, and made to strike his opponent again, who warded the blow off and gave him one on the jaw which fractured it.

Cockney was laid up for the rest of the voyage, and when we arrived in Queenstown he took action against the mate, who was fined five pounds and expenses. The captain was fined two pounds for not having made an entry regarding the matter in the official log.

Cockney had been in bad odour with the chief mate for a long time. He was a confirmed malcontent, and no one had any use for him. He reckoned that there was a " white rat " (tale-bearer) in the forecastle who carried yarns to the mate. He was at the wheel when the ship broached-to down off the Horn, and instead of making for the wheel again, the same as the other man did, he went deliberately into his bunk, where the mate found him. He would have made a good agitator for a trade union. He tried to stir up mischief on the second or third day he was on board, and kept it up all the time.

As the ship was still setting towards St. Paul Rocks, the two boats were lowered into the water with six men and an officer in each, and we started towing for all we were worth. There was still not a breath of wind, and the sea was as smooth as glass. We could see ten ships, nine away to the eastward of us and one about five miles to the westward of us. The heat from the sun was terrific, our necks and arms were blistered and scorched, while the sweat at the same time was running down our backs.

Several large sharks were about, nosing round the two boats. We used to strike them with the oars without any effect. The mate, however, reached over the stern with a boat-axe and sank the blade into the head of a big fellow about sixteen feet long. This fellow was thinking seriously at the time of making a jump at the mate. As soon as he received the blow from the axe he dived and left a streak of blood behind him.

At one time there must have been about twenty sharks around the two boats, but all of a sudden there was a scatter, and on looking into the water we saw a large fish about six feet below the surface. He was chasing the sharks. He was rather slow in his movements and could not keep up with them. This fish was about eight or nine feet long and about four and a half feet wide. The chief mate gave orders to have boat-axes ready in case they were needed, as the fish was what is known as the blanket fish, which sponge-divers often have to contend with round the Florida coast. From a diver's point of view they are the most dangerous fish in the sea. This fish passed away to the northward and we saw no more of him, and the sharks returned again after a while.

After rowing for about two hours the captain called us on board, as he saw a puff of wind on the water coming up from the south. The boats were lifted clear of the water and the yards were squared ready for the wind when it came. It came up slowly and the coolness from it was delicious. The sails began to draw, and we forged ahead enough to give the vessel steerage-way. The wind lasted for about an hour and a half and then died out again, as calm as before. We were then far enough ahead to clear St. Paul Rocks, which were about a mile astern as we drifted past them.

In the afternoon we could count twenty-five ships, all except one to the eastward of us, and several of them were hull down. About five o'clock in the afternoon a heavy rain squall came away from the north-west. It lasted for nearly two hours, and then died away again. This put us away towards the north-east and close up to a German vessel bound to Bremen with a cargo of rice from Rangoon. He reported that he and most of the vessels in sight had been becalmed in that vicinity for ten days. I was at the wheel at the time and overheard the captain say to the chief mate that there was a possibility of the Gaekwar being among this crowd yet. The chief mate looked upon this as being impossible, seeing that we had spent twenty-two days in Monte Video.

Calm prevailed all night until shortly after midnight, when another puff came away from the north-west which lasted until six o'clock in the morning, when we found ourselves surrounded by ships on all sides. The breeze seemed to have carried us right in among them when they must have been lying becalmed, and only about two miles away was our old friend the Gaekwar. He reported rounding the Horn five days later than us, and had fine weather all the way until abreast of the Falkland Islands, when he had a fresh blow from the north-west which lasted for four days. He sighted the same icebergs as we were among, but he was away twenty miles to the eastward and managed to keep clear of them all. He reported having six men who had never been to sea before, and having had to go under reduced sail most of the time.

For the next twenty-four hours we had a dead calm; the ship having gained only a mile and a half for the whole twenty-four hours. The Gaekwar was about four miles to the eastward of us. At four o'clock next morning the north-east trades came away fresh and at daylight the Gaekwar was right astern of us about six miles away, and kept in that position all day. During the next night the trade winds came away strong, about as much as we could stagger under with all sail set, and no ships were in sight. We came to the conclusion that we had left them all astern.

About a week after this we started to bend our hard-weather suit of sails, and to make all preparations for the hard wintry weather around the British coast. Our crew were now of the best, all good sailormen. We were only one man short, viz., Davis, the Cockney, who was laid up with a fractured jaw.

The men who were shipped at Monte Video turned out to be good men. Bob, the Cockney, had been a long time at sea and had spent his early days in the Blackwall frigate-built ships. He had also sailed on the Black Ball Line ships—the Donald Mackay, and James Baines. The latter vessel beat all records ever made by a sailing ship, having done 423 miles in twenty-four hours. Bob also had short spells on shore : he had been a hobo in America, a sundowner in Australia, a beach-comber in Rio de Janeiro and

Buenos Aires, and a hanger-on at Joe Beef's hotel in Montreal. He had been a chanteyman in Green's Blackwall ships, where he received ten shillings per month extra. He was well worth ten shillings per month extra, as he was the finest chanteyman I ever heard; he had a fine powerful voice.

We often had to clear hawse in Queenstown and our chanteying made the harbour ring. During fine weather Bob would give us an entertainment on the main hatch. He knew all the finest songs of the day; he was a splendid conjurer, step-dancer, boxer, and story-teller. He told us that he spent five months as a hobo in America, but that kind of life did not appeal to him, so he gave it up for a job as hanger-on at Joe Beef's hotel in Montreal. His duties were to make himself generally useful during the day, and entertain customers during the evening. The job was a fairly good one, but, like all sailormen, he had to get away to sea again after a few months.

His sundowning experience was more to his liking. He was one of those men who were called " Murrimbidgee Whalers," now called " Murrimbidgee Hums." They were called whalers because they used to catch fish in the Murrimbidgee River, and sell those that they could not eat to station hands, farmers, and publicans. They were called sundowners, owing to always striking a station about sundown, where they were also sure of getting a supper, bed, and breakfast for nothing. They seldom went any distance from the river. They would go up one side and come down along the other side.

Old Bob remarked that those whalers never did any work, except sometimes chop wood to the cook for his breakfast. They were always as fat as pigs, and, to use his own expression, they never needed to go and work at a station to get their kidneys lined. He became a beach-comber in Rio through having been left in hospital sick. When he came out of hospital he went to the British Consul, who held a few pounds which were due him. He only had this money for a few hours, owing to his pockets being picked. After a couple of weeks he was turned out of the boarding house and had to sleep anywhere. The rice wharf at the Gambo sheltered him for a while.

As the yellow fever season was fast approaching, he managed to stow away in a cattle-boat bound to Buenos Aires. The port lands at Buenos Aires were the favourite camping grounds for beach-combers at that time. They used to burrow like rabbits into a bank about five feet high, which afforded them good shelter from all weathers. The captain of the port's office was near at hand, where they all used to get coffee and biscuits at six o'clock in the morning from the vigilantes. I was in Buenos Aires many years afterwards, and I noticed that the vigilantes still supplied the beach-combers with coffee in the morning. The captain of the port is a man of great authority in all seaports in South America, and is generally an ex-naval officer holding the rank of captain or commander, according to the size of the port. All disputes or trouble of any kind must be reported to the captain of the port, who sometimes arbitrates between disputants. If trouble arises among crews of ships lying in the harbour, he sends his vigilantes off to arrest the men if the captain of the ship requests them to do so.

Flood, the Irishman, told us that he had been arrested by the vigilantes in Iquique and sent to prison for seven days. Before he received his breakfast he had to break a cartload of stones for road metal. There was no scamping over this job, as all the metal had to pass through holes in an iron plate. Prisoners who were not very expert at the job were let out of their cells at five o'clock in the morning so that they could manage to have all the metal disposed of before eight o'clock. At nine o'clock they had to go into the chain gang to sweep streets and clean closets out. No useless prisoners were kept in South American jails at that time.

Confirmed criminals were not allowed loose on society for long, especially those who were classed as *muy mal hombres* (very bad men). They were either poisoned when they went back to prison a second time or else shot by the police, who declared they had to do it in self-defence. A Brazilian Government official declared to me that some men in that country who were born criminals, could never go straight, and had no right to be allowed to prey on society. Consequently, it was only right that such men should be disposed of by the police.

BULLY MARTIN.

ONE morning when we were in what are called the "horse latitudes," we were overhauled by a four-masted Loch Line ship. The wind was light—only about a three-knot breeze for us. The Loch Liner was doing about a good knot more an hour. Our captain got into a blue funk when he came up and was informed that the vessel was overhauling us so quickly. Orders were given to sweat up every sail fore and aft.

About an hour and a half was spent sweating up, but still the Loch Liner came up on us as fast as ever. About ten o'clock he was up alongside us, and commenced signalling. He was sixty-one days out from Melbourne, laden with wool, and bound for London. He was, of course, flying light, whilst we were deeply loaded, and we could see when he rolled away from us that he was fairly clean under water, whilst we had quite a heavy marine growth on our sides. Our chief mate pointed all this out to our captain, who was getting awfully riled at the idea of any ship passing us. The beating of the Gaekwar five days down to the Horn must have had a bad effect on him. After that, he seemed to think that nothing could pass us. This, however, was an eye-opener. "I guess," said he, "that there packet will find out that we can show a clean pair of heels as soon as the wind freshens up."

The vessel was quite close to us now. The chief mate, who was scanning the ship's poop with the telescope, remarked that the captain was a heavily-built man with a reddish beard, large nose and rugged features. "I don't know any of those Loch Line captains," our "Old Man" remarked, "but I have heard of one with a reputation as a hard sail carrier known as Bully Martin."

Ralph Wiberg, the Swede, who was making the flags up on the poop at the time, remarked in an undertone to the chief mate that the man on that ship was Bully Martin. The chief mate informed the captain of the fact. "I guess," said our captain, "that he is a foeman worthy of my steel, while I must admit we have not much

chance against a ship that is flying light and has a clean bottom."
At sunset that night he was away ahead of us hull down; the wind
at the time was a nine-knot breeze from the north-east.

Bully Martin was the best known master mariner on the seven
seas. Unlike Bully Forbes, he was a silent, tenacious man, with
an iron constitution, iron nerve, and iron will. Bully Forbes was
a brilliant man of quick decision, but went under with the loss of
the Schomberg, and eventually sank into obscurity. Prosperity
turned his head, and so also did adversity.

Not so Bully Martin, who never became inflated with his own
importance, and never would, even if he had commanded the
finest ship afloat. He was called Bully Martin because he was a
bully—a man-driver and a ship-driver as well. He started his first
command in a small vessel and rose step by step until he commanded one of the finest four-masted vessels afloat. His first
command was in the days of wooden ships and iron men. He was
a very hard man on his crews; no one ever cared to make a second
voyage with him before the mast.

This man could not be considered as a man of a mercurial
temperament, nothing seemed to elate or depress him; and although
he was a shipmaster for about forty years, it is said that he never
cost the underwriters a farthing. It is also said that he took a short
spell ashore as examiner of masters and mates in Calcutta, and
during the time he held that position there were no passes—everyone was found to be incompetent. Officers who sailed with him
always considered him to be a navigator and seaman of the first
order, and second to none.

Our captain, a reputed bully, had been very mild during the
whole passage from 'Frisco, and he proved himself to be a man
with an iron constitution and iron nerve. He never seemed to get
tired. The steward informed us that the captain had gone six days
without sleep down off the Horn, and that he never tasted drink at
sea. The chief mate we found to be a very fair man, and seemed
latterly to have a great influence with the captain, probably through
being an expert navigator.

If we were sailing exactly under the same conditions as the
Loch Liner, it was very doubtful if we could pass her, as our

vessel was too tender through being so loftily-rigged and over-sparred. Next morning the wind was strong from the north-east, and we were diving bows under, throwing the spray as high as the fore lower topsail yard, and doing ten knots. Every stitch was set, which was as much as we could stagger under. The Loch Liner was out of sight, but a large three-masted ship was on our lee bow with his royals and fore and mizzen topgallant sails fast. In less than an hour we were up alongside him. He turned out to be the Malaysia, of Liverpool. He took no notice of our hard driving, but kept going as he did when he first sighted us. He left San Francisco before us, and must have made a long passage. About two in the afternoon the Malaysia was out of sight astern.

During the next night the wind hauled round to the south-east and afterwards to the south, and remained there all next day. Then it started to rain, and the wind shifted to the south-west and blew very hard—a very heavy sea came rolling up. During a heavy squall that night the wind suddenly shifted from right aft to right ahead. We were struck flat aback with squared yards. The ship put her stern right under. She had so much sternway that the man at the wheel was nearly washed away. The island of Flores, one of the Azores, was only about fifty miles away at the time. The ship had to be snugged down, but several new sails were lost that night. We heard afterwards that the Malaysia lost four men overboard that night, and several others had to go to hospital on arrival at Queenstown.

The Malaysia disappeared about five years after this incident, and my own ship which I am now writing of, went down some-where in the same vicinity. The same captain was not in her when she disappeared. A young Scotsman had her then, and he was also a hard driver. She was seen by another ship just before dark carrying a heavy press of sail. The weather was bad, with every appearance of a heavy gale coming on, and the barometer was low. This happened about ten or eleven years after I was in her. I only saw her once after I left her, and that was off Cape Horn, when I was in command of a three-masted full-rigged ship called the Albuera. We were both beating to the westward, and as usual she was being terribly over-driven.

IN PORT.

IT was the captain's original intention to call at Falmouth for
orders, but he decided later on that Queenstown would be the
more suitable port, so we made for the latter.   On the night before
our arrival at Queenstown we nearly ran down a large outward
ship, head-reaching under topsails and foresail.   The young Swede
was on the lookout, and never saw the vessel until we were almost
on the top of her.   The second mate was the first to see her.   We
passed so close to her that a biscuit could have been thrown on her
poop.

Next morning we hove to, to take the Queenstown pilot on
board, and at noon we were anchored in Queenstown Harbour.

Cockney Davis went along to the captain as soon as the anchor
was down, to inform him that he must be supplied with a boat to
take him ashore to see the shipping master, as he had a charge to
lay against the chief mate.   The charge was assault and battery
on the high seas.   Cockney had been figuring on receiving a fairly
good sum of money as compensation.   Nothing less than fifty
pounds would please him ; he reckoned that any judge would award
him that amount.   If the mate was willing to come to terms out
of court, he would consider the matter and let him off with sixty
pounds.

The captain and the pilot were still on the poop directing
operations when Cockney came aft.   I was engaged in reeling up
the deep-sea lead-line at the time and heard all that passed.

Cockney came up on the poop with a truculent look on.
" Begging your parding, capting," said he, " you know what my
business is."

" I know nothing about your business, you insolent-looking
hound of a sea-lawyer—get down off my poop before you get
kicked down, you low-down, back street Cockney."

Cockney became more truculent in appearance than ever.   He
held up his forefinger as a warning.   " Now, capting, I warn you

strite, that if you don't listen to my compl'int, you won't be mawster of this ere ship long; that's me, Bill Dives from Shadwell, and Ratcliffe 'Ighway at that."

The captain took him by the shoulder and pushed him down the poop ladder, and then Cockney's "Billingsgate" came out strong. "You blawsted blue-nose of a skipper, I'll fix you and your bleeding blue-nose of a chief mite. Strike me lucky if I don't, struth!"

The captain and the pilot walked to the afterpart of the poop so that they should not hear the foul-mouthed villain. The second mate, however, came along, caught him by the shoulders and ran him along the deck right up to the forecastle door. After the second mate went aft, Cockney came out of the forecastle, went up on the forecastle-head to where the chief mate was standing, and demanded to have a boat put out so that he could go ashore and lay his case before the shipping master. As the mate was very busy at the time, he put Cockney off by stating that he would attend to him later on.

This remark seemed to please Cockney, as he told some of the men that the mate looked a bit scared and would be glad to square him with a fairly good sum of money. Cockney intended to engage what he called a loryer (lawyer), but if the mate was prepared to capitulate, lawyers' expenses would be saved.

There was no capitulation on the mate's part. Cockney was told that a shore boat at the gangway would take him ashore, and that he had to be on board at seven o'clock. "Don't worry about me, Mister Mite," said the Cockney. "I'll be back and you'll know all about my commin' when I do come; that's me, strite."

As soon as our anchor was down we were surrounded by boats, and the captain was surrounded by men with cards in their hands and testimonials from other captains. Tall fellows would try to reach over shorter fellows' heads. "Sure, captain," one would call out, "you are not meaning to go past me, who has known you fer so many years; I sarved you only two years ago."

"Shut up, you ould fool," said a tall, young man; "my name is Fitzgerald, a man known all over as a straight-going and thorough business man : sure, every captain knows me."

Fitzgerald got the business. He came into the forecastle when we were sitting at dinner. "Bhoys," said he, "I am sure yez have all heard of me—Fitzgerald, the best master tailor in the South of Ireland. Sure, I only got married last wake, and I am still in good humour and throwing suits of clothing away almost for nothing, just by way of celebrating the evint." The boys all gathered round him to look at his samples of ready-made clothing.

Ralph the Swede knew him, and told him so. "And were you satisfied wid the suit that I supplied you?" "Yes," said Ralph, "it was as good a suit as I ever had." "Thank you, sorr," said Fitzgerald, "you're a gintleman." As Ralph's opinion carried a lot of weight in the forecastle, Fitzgerald did fairly well.

The men reckoned that it was the proper time to buy clothes when they had a good fellow like Fitzgerald to deal with, and besides, remarked some of them, it is nice to have a new suit to walk ashore in. Others would say that it was far better to deal with an Irishman than with a dirty old Jew.

Fitzgerald heard this remark and felt rather elated over it. "Sure, bhoys," said he, "yez all know that an Oirishman never has any use for a Jew. When my ould uncle was dying he asked his rivirince to make sure that he was buried in a Jewish cemetery. His rivirince, the praist, was horrified and asked my ould uncle if he had taken laive of his sinses. 'Och, no, father,' said he. 'Me raison for that is that the divil would never come to look for me if Oi was buried in a Jewish saimitry.'"

Cockney Charlie wanted a pair of Queenstown-made seaboots, but Fitzgerald had to send to a shoemaker for them. Ould Andy, his boatman, was called along. "See here, Andy," said Fitzgerald, "I want you to go ashore to Misther O'Sullivan for a pair of leather seaboots, size ten for a nine fut." Andy obeyed, and slid down a rope into his boat, but about ten minutes afterwards, when he was some distance away from the ship, he turned and came back alongside again. When he came into the forecastle, Mr. Fitzgerald exclaimed, "What is the matter, Andy?" "Och, sure," said Andy, "I clane forgot the sizes. Was it a nine boot for a ten fut, or was it a ten boot for a nine fut?" "H—l roast ye!"exclaimed Fitzgerald. "I tould ye to git a ten boot. Never mind the fut;

get ashore at once, and don't take any more drink, you drunken ould divil that ye are." Ould Andy put a look of dismay on. "Sure, Misther Fitzgerald, I have only had one little drop today." "What is that you have rolled in paper under your arm? Is it a bottle for whisky?" "Sure, Misther Fitzgerald, that is a bit of salt bafe I am taking ashore to my daughter's childer." About two hours afterward Ould Andy returned with the seaboots and more than half seas over. "You drunken ould baist," said Fitzgerald, "I will sack ye." "Oh, Sints presarve me! Misther Fitzgerald, I am as sober as ye are, and so I am."

Mrs. Williams was the bumboat woman, and those of us who did not patronise Fitzgerald went in for big licks in the food line—especially condensed milk. She told us that her husband had been blind for many years and could do nothing for himself, which necessitated her going into the bumboat business, in addition to running a shall shop.

Cockney did not return to the ship at the time stipulated by the chief mate; it was seven or eight o'clock before he returned, pretty well under the influence of liquor. He told us that he had consulted his loryer, who reckoned that he had a good case, and that he was going to get nearly one hundred pounds in compensation, and that the chief mate would also get three months. His loryer was thinking seriously of charging the mate with attempted murder on the high seas. As I was an eye-witness I was to be called to give evidence; also three other men. On the following day the captain and chief mate had to appear at the court, and were fined two pounds and five pounds respectively, and Cockney received no compensation.

After lying four days at Queenstown we received orders to proceed to Liverpool. A powerful tug came for us the next day to tow us to that port, and the order was given to "man the windlass." As we walked merrily round the capstan Cockney Bob was at his best. His first chantey was:

> "We are homeward bound for Liverpool town,
>   Good-bye, fare ye well, good-bye, fare ye well;
> Homeward bound for Liverpool town,
>   Hoo-rah, my boys, we are homeward bound."
>   Etc., etc.

The weather was fairly good, and we anchored for the last time in the Mersey in about twenty-six hours after leaving Queenstown.

As we hove up anchor that afternoon we fairly made the Mersey ring with our chanteying. Cockney Bob started with " Leave her, Johnnie, leave her ":

> " I thought I heard our captain say,
> Leave her, Johnnie, leave her,
> Come along and get your pay;
> Leave her, Johnnie, leave her.
> " Times are hard and wages low,
> Leave her, Johnnie, leave her;
> A hungry ship and a drunken crew,
> Leave her, Johnnie, leave her."
> Etc., etc.

Another chantey was " Sally Brown ":

> " Oh, Sally Brown was a bright Mulatto,
> She drinks rum and chews tobacco;
> Spend my money on Sally Brown,
> Way hay, roll and go."
> Etc., etc.

As soon as we entered the lock our decks were crowded with men, Custom House officers, Board of Trade men, men who called themselves riggers, boarding-house runners, Jewish tailors, carriers, porters, marine store dealers, dealers in slush who wished to strike a bargain with the cook for his grease, and, last but not least, crooks and loafers. They all seemed so glad to see us back, although many of us had never been in the port of Liverpool before!

The riggers, however, pretended to have the first claim on us, with the object of working in our places and thus allowing us to get away from the ship at once. It was then a Liverpool custom that those men who called themselves riggers jumped on board a deep-water sailing ship as soon as she entered the lock, with the object of getting employed as substitutes. Usually, every sailor-man employs one of those men to take his place for five shillings. The sailor takes the rigger along to the chief mate, who takes the names of both men.

The riggers seemed to be absolutely starving. As it was our last meal on board, most of our dinner was left standing about the forecastle in mess kids, and when they came into the forecastle and saw the food standing about, they cut the salt horse up in pieces with their sheath knives and tore the meat off the bones like wild animals. The maggoty and weevily biscuits were eaten with great relish—maggots, weevils and all. The sailors who did not wish to remain in Liverpool went straight away by Board of Trade to their respective destinations.

When the substitutes had been engaged, all hands went into the forecastle to put the finishing touch on their packing up; but, alas, some crooks had already collared some of our belongings during the time we were on the quarter-deck arranging with the chief mate regarding substitutes. Before leaving, I took one last look at the forecastle, and then aloft where I had spent many a hard hour hanging on by my eyebrows, reefing, goose-winging, or furling sails down in the Southern Ocean with nothing but a foot-rope to stand on, whilst the ship was rolling over fifty degrees to leeward.

Before leaving the ship's side I could not resist the temptation of jumping on board again to bid the two officers good-bye. The chief mate was on the forecastle-head, and hard blue-nose that he was supposed to be, he shook me heartily by the hand. " Good-bye my lad," said he, " you are made of the right material and sure to get on. Next time I meet you I expect to find you living in the other end of the ship. I have no advice to offer you, as you do not need any; so good-bye again."

The second mate was on the poop, and as soon as I reached the top of the ladder I ran up against the captain. " Hallo, my lad," said he, " you are a free man once more." I blurted out that I had come to bid the second mate good-bye. " Wall," said the captain, " that sure is very good of you; but did you expect to find me? " I replied that I would not have trespassed on his poop if I had known that he was there. " That is all right; you are the right sort, you are sure to get on. Always put your right foot foremost, as you have done here. And if you are ever in port with me again, be sure and look me up; I will be glad to see you—so good-bye, and good luck to you."

As we drove up the dock in the Sailors' Home cart a strange feeling of actual loneliness came over me as I took a last look at the ship which had braved so many storms, icebergs, and hard driving during the time that I was in her, and as I realised that there was a spot of kindness somewhere under the hard exteriors of the blue-nose captain and mate.

I have little more to relate. We were paid off at the shipping office two days afterwards, when I left Liverpool for Glasgow.

We arrived at Liverpool on the same day that the Gaekwar arrived at Falmouth, which was a great beating for that vessel. Our captain won his bet. The Loch Liner (Bully Martin's ship) arrived at London the day after our arrival at Queenstown.

As I have already mentioned, our gallant ship went down south of the Azores one stormy winter's night with all hands. Our captain had left her two or three voyages before that to take over the command of a large four-master, and, like many more of us, he finally went into steam.

The chief mate made one more voyage in that ship, and then got command of a large three-master. He went into steam also, but had to start as second mate. I believe that he was in command of a steamer only eighteen months afterwards.

The second mate I met in Rio de Janeiro in 1896. He was then in command of a large four-masted barque, and I was in command of a Glasgow ship which had formerly been a passenger ship in the Australian trade.

The men who manned the ship during the voyage I have just described, I suppose are dead long ago. The sailors of those days lived very short lives. When they reached forty-five they were considered too old for the strenuous life on a sailing ship. Hard work, poor food, discontent, sickly climates, wore a sailorman's life out very quickly. He was an old man long before his time.

The crimps and boarding-house keepers flourished for many years after, until 1900, when the three months' advance was considered illegal. They have had their day, their nefarious methods of making a living are a thing of the past. The present-day sailor is a steamboat man, well housed, well paid, and well fed. He belongs to a union run on reasonable lines. If he has a reasonable grievance he reports it to his union, which takes the matter up with the employers and everything is settled amicably. There is no ill-feeling between the Seamen's Union and the shipowner of the present day.

> Old Stormalong has gone to rest,
> Of all the sailors he was the best;
> We'll dig his grave with a silver spade,
> And lower him down with a golden chain—
>   By all his shipmates blest.
> To my aye, aye, Mister Stormalong.
>   Etc., etc.

AN UNDISCIPLINED SHIP.

IT was in the stormy month of February, 1885, that I sailed from the Queen's Dock, Glasgow, bound to Sydney, New South Wales, in a fine new ship on her maiden voyage. We were ordered on board at six in the morning, but none of us turned up before nine. The vessel was lying about ten feet away from the wharf and the stevedores were still putting cargo on board when we came down. There were only two men in the forecastle when I arrived. One of them told me he was going in the ship and that the other man was his brother who was seeing him off. I was offered a drink out of a half-mutchkin bottle, but declined to take any.

The sailorman informed me that he came from some street off Paisley Road, that his name was Carmichael, and that he had been engaged as a rigger bending the ship's sails before signing on. He held up the whisky bottle, and smilingly remarked that there was plenty of that good stuff in the ship. He knew where it was all stowed, and he looked forward to having a good time on the voyage out to Sydney. The whisky, he said, was stowed in the 'tween deck from the pump casing right aft to the bulkhead. There was also beer in the lower hold forward. He had taken a mental note where the valuable cargo was stowed also.

About half past nine more men turned up, and all had about as much " in " as they could carry. A well-known boarding-master from the Broomielaw brought four men down, and saw that their clothes were placed in the forecastle. As usual, each man received his stock of refreshments from the boarding-house keeper and any balance of money due him.

About 11 a.m. the cargo was all in, and hatches were put on by the stevedores. One plank, about a foot wide, still remained out for a gangway, and as one sailorman was coming on board over it with his bag on his shoulder he overbalanced himself owing to the quantity of liquor he had " in." The bag fell into the dock and the man fell backwards with a flop on to the plank. A boatman who

122

happened to be passing, rowed his boat between the ship and the wharf and picked the bag up.

A fairly large number of people had assembled on the quay to see the ship off. A very stout, pompous-looking old gentleman brought his son down. He asked for the captain as he wished to introduce the young man to him, and expressed a wish to have a look round the vessel, seeing that his son was going away in her as an apprentice. The chief mate ordered another plank to be put out between the ship and the wharf so that no one would be likely to fall into the water. The old gentleman and his son managed to get on board, and the latter was introduced to the chief mate.

" This is my son Albert," said the old gentleman. " I am sure he will make a good sailor; he loves the water and spends a lot of time on it."

" If weight can make a sailor," said the mate, " he ought to be a good one. What weight is he, anyway? "

The old gentleman replied that his son was thirteen stones twelve pounds, and was fifteen years of age.

The mate gave a sort of sneering laugh as he looked the young man all over. He was dressed in a light grey Newmarket ulster, with hat and grey spats to match. Another young seaman and I were engaged in passing some small stores into the saloon at the time and heard all this conversation, to our great amusement. As the captain was engaged at the time, the old gentleman had to wait for the time being.

Three other apprentices came out of the half-deck with their new uniforms on, and on seeing them the old gentleman became anxious to see his son with his new uniform on also. He came over and asked me where his son's clothes were, as he wanted to see how he looked on board ship. I asked him if he was sure that his son's clothes were on board. He replied that he sent them down at seven o'clock that morning. I advised them to go to the half-deck and see for themselves.

About half an hour later the young man appeared on deck in his new uniform, and looked about as portly as his father when the Newmarket ulster was off; his cheeks bulged out like the stern of a Dutch galiot, and his double chin lay in a fold over the top of his three-inch collar. He gazed up aloft, looked over the side, and up aloft again; then the mate came along and ordered him to get his working clothes on and turn to at once.

The young fellow who was helping me to pass the stores into the saloon, a man by the name of Davidson, and I, were the only sober men forward. Some lay where they fell on deck, and the Board of Trade man had great difficulty in getting their names. One Cockney, in his bunk, was trying to sing " Go and leave me if you wish it " in real Cockney pot-house style; an Irishman from Drogheda was singing the " Rose of Tralee " at the same time. The man who boasted that he knew where all the drink was stowed, and his friend also, were lying speechless on the forecastle floor, and two empty half-mutchkin bottles beside them. One young fellow from Kelvinhaugh tried hard to get ashore after the planks were taken away. He was starting to take his clothes off for a swim when I pulled him down off the spare spar. He said that he wanted to get ashore to bid good-bye to some girls he knew, who were standing on the quay throwing kisses to him. The Board of Trade man found that we were two men short at sailing time. Four riggers had to be engaged to assist in taking the ship down to the Tail of the Bank, owing to so many men being drunk.

The pilot was stationed on the forecastle-head along with the mate. The tug took our towrope, orders were given to " let go all aft," the tug put a strain on our towline, and our voyage commenced. Several people followed us along the quay to the pier-heads, apparently to see the last of some friend, sweetheart, or relative who was lying dead to the world in the forecastle. The weather was not promising; there was every appearance of a strong blow. Being sober, I was sent to the wheel, and there I had to remain for three and a half hours.

When at the wheel I saw the captain for the first time. The captain who signed us on at the shipping office (we found out afterwards) resigned and another had taken his place. The new captain was a man over fifty years of age, and had the appearance of a Billy Boy skipper. He was a thick-set man, with a long, straggling beard. Some of the men called him " Old Buntline Stops," and others called him " Old Tackity Whiskers." His appearance was not prepossessing by any means.   He was slovenly in dress, whether in port or at sea.   He, to all appearances, was not a fit man to take command of such a vessel.   He was an uneducated man, and spoke with a strong Cockney accent, leaving out his " h's " where required and putting them in where they were not required.

We towed straight to the Gareloch, where our compasses were to be adjusted on the following day.   When nearing the anchorage the carpenter was told to stand by the windlass, and when the order " Let go the anchor " was given, the carpenter opened the patent windlass up and let the chain rip.   The mate and the pilot bawled out " Hold on the cable " several times.   The windlass was not fitted with a brake; the compressor had to serve both purposes. The carpenter, unfortunately, had jammed the compressor, and the chain ran out to the last link.   The end of the chain, of course, was fastened in the chain-locker.   This left us in a fine old fix; nearly 120 fathoms of cable had run out on the top of the anchor. The compressor had to be released, and all hands who were sober were ordered to man the windlass to heave in cable.   The tug had to hold us in position until the cable was hove in, and the anchor sighted, in case it was foul.   This job took us an hour and a half. Luckily the anchor was not foul, so we let it go again.   The carpenter either did not understand the windlass or else he was drunk.

The riggers were still on board.   Had it not been for them we would never have managed to raise the anchor, as most of the crew were still lying drunk in the forecastle.   The towrope was hauled in, and the tug came alongside to take the four riggers ashore to Greenock, where they could take train to Glasgow.   The four men marched aft for their pay.   The captain offered them five shillings each, whilst they claimed ten shillings each and their fare from Greenock to Glasgow.   The riggers contended that as soon as the anchor was dropped their contract was finished.   The heaving up of the anchor was extra work, and took an hour and a half.   The " Old Man " again offered them five shillings each, saying he would not give one penny more, and ordered them out of the ship.

The captain proceeded to write out an order to be presented for payment to the owners of the ship, who were in Glasgow.   It took him nearly half an hour to do so. The men were anxious to get away, the tug was blowing her steam whistle, and at last the " Old Man " came out with four pieces of paper, one of which he handed to each man. He told them that he had split the difference ; the orders were made out for seven and sixpence. The men refused to agree to this : ten shillings they wanted, and ten shillings they were going to have. The pilot came along and the men asked his opinion. He told them that it was no business of his, but, at the same time, he considered that they should get the ten shillings and leave out the ninepence train fare from Greenock to Glasgow.

The " Old Man " eventually agreed to write out an order to each man for ten shillings. The mate was standing close by and the men suggested that he should write the orders out and the captain sign them, as they did not like the idea of having to wait another half hour or more, as they would eventually lose their train to Glasgow. I was standing by aft to let go the towboat's ropes, and saw and heard the whole performance.

The " Old Man," mate, and pilot, all went into the saloon, and during the time they were in, the riggers showed me the seven and sixpenny orders which the captain had made out. I never saw such scrawls. One of the riggers declared that it was like lifting a bluebottle fly out of an inkwell and dropping it on a sheet of paper.

In less than ten minutes the mate came out with the four orders and handed them to the men—all signed by the captain. The men read them over carefully and were satisfied. As they stood reading them over, the captain came out and called them " imposters," " Jews," and " wharf rats," and pointing to the tug alongside, he roared out, " Now, 'oof it, you d——— rascals." He meant " hoof it." The men took no more notice of him, but went on board the tug. I let go the ropes, the tug tooted her steam whistle for good-night, and disappeared in the darkness.

Before I went forward, I remarked to the mate that the men would do fairly well out of the transaction, as they had two orders each, viz., one for seven shillings and sixpence and one for ten shillings, which would amount to seventeen shillings and sixpence for each man. Seeing the tug had left, I went forward to the forecastle to get some tea. I had scarcely started to tea when the second mate came along and stated that the captain wanted me. I had a pretty good idea what I was wanted for, as the mate would have told the captain that the riggers still had the seven-and-six-penny orders in their possession.

When I went into the saloon the " Old Man " was sitting at the table.   " Here, you young bounder," he roared out, " have you been working 'and in glove with them there riggers? Are you trying to do me? I'll make you pay for that extra thirty shillings which I gave those men."

I replied that I had nothing to do with it; it was no affair of mine : " and besides," I said, " you cannot keep that off my wages."

On hearing this, he fairly turned purple, and, pointing to the door, he roared out, " You thief of a sea-lawyer, get out of my cabin at once, 'oof it."

I cleared out at once and did not need a second bidding. The man was both drunk and mad.

Next day we started work at daylight getting everything ready for sea, and later on the compass adjuster came on board and started adjusting the compasses.

When this operation was finished, we hove up anchor and were towed to the Tail of the Bank to take in twenty tons of powder. Three of our men remained in their bunks all day sleeping off the drink.   The captain and officers seemed to take no notice of this breach of discipline.   Several others went away to have long smokes.

Two pier-head jumpers were brought on board in the evening. One was a Yankee by the name of Gleeson, and the other man was a Welshman.

The four apprentices were all first voyagers, and had a bewildered look at themselves in dongarees and seaboots, and with new belts and sheath-knives on their hips.   The second mate took them to wash the decks down; a sailorman and I did the pumping. Two boys had to do the scrubbing, and the other two carried the buckets of water along to the second mate.   The fat boy, Albert, got very fatigued, and considered that half a bucketful was enough to carry along the deck.   The second mate, however, had a different opinion; fat Albert had to fill his bucket up.

On the previous night when we were anchored in the Gareloch, I was keeping my anchor watch from eight to ten. I went into the half-deck to see how the boys were getting on, and found that they were all very enthusiastic over the new profession they had taken up, except fat Albert, who could not see how he was going to exist on the small amount of food they got for dinner and tea. During the short time I was in their room he had eaten two large biscuits. I asked him how he came to be so fat and yet so young. He could not account for it, he said; supposed it was his growth. His people at home did not think he ate much. He told me that he used to drink from six to ten bottles of stout some days, which probably would be partly the means of putting some flesh on. His father had three public houses in London, and was considered to be well off. This boy was nicknamed " Jumbo " later on, and was never called by any other name for the rest of the voyage. Before we were a month out, he showed us that he could take his belt in six holes and was probably eleven stones in weight.

The oldest boy was a Scottish lad by the name of Jarvis, who turned out to be a strong, active lad. He had spent two years in the Conway training ship and had only three years' apprenticeship to put in, whilst the others had the full four years.

Next to Jarvis was Clarke, an English boy, son of a Church of England minister, and like some ministers' sons he turned out to be a very rowdy lad after he had been at sea for a couple of months. It appeared that he had been kept too much under restraint at home, and when he found himself among a lot of rowdy men in a badly-disciplined ship, he showed every sign of turning out to be a hard case. He chewed tobacco, smoked, and swore as much as the oldest sailor in the forecastle. Had he found himself on board a well-disciplined ship he would have turned out to be a very smart lad.

Next to Clarke was a Scottish lad by the name of Nisbet, from Inverness-shire. He was the smallest, and was called the " Nipper."

When we started to load the powder at the Tail of the Bank all fires and lights had to be put out right fore and aft the ship. An inspector came round and examined every man's stock of matches, as only safety matches were allowed. Each man was supplied with a pair of india-rubber shoes before he went into the hold to stow the powder. A magazine was built in the main hatchway, and the powder came on board in strong wooden kegs fastened with copper nails.

On the following day we signalled for the tug. The weather was fine for a winter's day, and the wind was southerly. When the tug came off, the towrope was passed on board, and the windlass was manned to the tune of "Rio Grande." The anchor was hove up and we started on the "long trail." When we were well down the Firth of Clyde we commenced to set sail. The wind was south, which prevented us trying to pass through the Irish Channel, so we had to shape a course for the North Channel instead. When all sail was set, all hands had to clap on to the towrope and haul it in. The tug then came close to and passed his heaving-line on board, with a bag attached to hold all the ship's letters and the usual bottle of whisky.

The night was now getting dark and rainy, and some of the oldest hands remarked that we should have a blow before long from the south-west, and later on from the north-west. Towards midnight the wind freshened up, with heavy rain, and all hands were called out to shorten sail. By three in the morning we were down to two lower topsails and full foresail. At daybreak the wind shifted to the north-west during a heavy squall and caught us flat aback. As the ship was under small sail we did not mind it very much. Yards were trimmed on the starboard tack, and a course set for going down the Irish Channel, which was more suitable than going to the North of Ireland at all times.

The watches were picked shortly after the tug left us. I was in the second mate's watch. The crew consisted of twelve able seamen, four apprentices, bos'n, sailmaker, carpenter, cook, steward, captain and two mates—twenty-four all told—and four stowaways who turned up when we were passing Corsewall Point. No one forward had seen the captain since the tug left us, and the man who was at the wheel at that time reckoned that the "Old Man" was drunk. Sailormen, naturally, take no notice of one of their own cloth getting drunk, but when it is a captain or an officer they despise him right away. They have no further use for him.

The chief mate was a little fat man from Aberdeenshire, about 29 years of age, quite pompous, and well pleased with himself, but nobody else was pleased with him, as we were not many days at sea before he was looked upon as being incompetent and a poor navigator.

The second mate was a big, rawboned man from Dundee way, about 26 years of age, and a fairly good second mate as far as abilities were concerned, but he made himself too cheap to the forward hands, and had not the slightest idea of maintaining discipline. So far as discipline was concerned, the captain and chief mate were equally as bad as the second mate. Any officer who cannot maintain discipline is not fit for executive duties; he is just as bad as an arrogant, overbearing officer.

The men forward used to call the second mate " Big Rory O'More "—not exactly to his face but within his hearing. We had not been a fortnight at sea before we became the most undisciplined lot of men afloat, and every man was a law unto himself ; even the apprentice boys, who were first voyagers, became saucy with the officers after a while. The second mate even went so far as to have a yarn with the man at the wheel occasionally.

When the men were called out to trim sail they grumbled. At eight bells, instead of mustering all the men and either counting them, or calling each man's name out, the man who was to relieve the wheel would call out, " The watch is aft "; the officer on the poop would call out, " Relieve the wheel and look-out "; whilst all the rest of the watch would probably still be in their bunks.

Gleeson, the American, and I got into bad odour over this business. We used to criticise this laxity of discipline, while the others argued that Jack was as good as his master, the only difference being that one lived aft and the other lived forward. Most of the men knew better, although they would not admit it.

Four of the crew came from Glasgow, and I have always found that Glasgow and Greenock men—with the exception of negroes—are the most difficult lot of men in the world to deal with. There are, of course, Glasgow men and Glasgow men. There are plenty of good men belonging to Glasgow, respectably brought up, men who make good at sea.

The four stowaways hailed from Glasgow; one of them was Carmichael's brother, who had the half-mutchkin bottle. The other three were typical Glasgow corner boys. Carmichael's brother maintained that he was too drunk to get ashore when the ship sailed, and he never intended to stowaway—a yarn that no one believed. The stowaways went aft to report themselves, and the mate told them that he would put them on board the first homeward bound ship that turned up.

Sweeney, the Irishman who sang the " Rose of Tralee," found himself " done in the eye," as he called it; he had a bagful of clothes, the contents of which were women's and children's wearing apparel. When coming across in the Irish boat to Glasgow he noticed lying alongside of his own sailor's bag another sailor's bag about double the size of his own. He considered this a splendid chance of getting a good outfit, and as soon as the vessel got alongside the quay in Glasgow he collared the large bag and jumped ashore. He opened the bag when he sobered up at the Tail of the Bank, and found that there was not a vestige of clothing in that bag of any use to him. He was without clothes, except what he stood up in.

The bos'n was a Norwegian and a good sailorman.

The cook turned out to be a dirty, lazy man. He was a Dutchman of some kind, and was nicknamed " Old Slushy."

The steward was a West Indian negro—fairly good-looking for a negro. When leaving Glasgow, three good-looking young women were seeing him off. One, he said, was his wife and the other two were her sisters. I noticed he took a very affectionate farewell of them, which was very amusing to us who were sober. He promised faithfully to write first " ortoonity."

AN ORGY IN THE FORECASTLE.

THE weather settled down quite fine after the wind shifted to the north-west. All sail was set, and we ran down along the Irish Coast in smooth water, doing about four knots. At about three in the afternoon we felt the vessel bump slightly not far from the Saltees. It must have been a sandbank as the pumpwell was sounded and no water found. The chief mate was on duty at the time.

Everything went well until about nine o'clock that evening when the wind backed into the south-west and came away strong. All hands were called out to shorten sail, and we were again under lower topsails and foresail. The wind was now a dead muzzler and blowing hard. We began shipping heavy seas on board, and one exceptionally heavy one smashed up a beautiful teakwood pig pen, the whole going over the side, taking three pigs over with it. One of the men got his leg broken later on.

As the captain had never been seen on deck since the tug left us in the Firth of Clyde, we all came to the conclusion that he was drunk and dead to the world. In the channel in winter time the captain of a ship is scarcely ever off the poop.

About five o'clock on the following morning my watch was called out to secure the masts, spars, and rigging. The mate had gone into a blue funk owing to the parrel of the main upper topsail yard carrying away. He evidently got it into his head that we would soon be dismasted. The mate's watch was aloft on the main securing the topsail-yard with wire lashings around the main topmast. When we came on deck we had to frap the rigging, owing to it having slackened up so much through being a new ship.

The wind went back into the north-west again and blew hard, with terrific hail squalls. We expected the chief mate to put the ship on the starboard tack and head down Channel. Instead of doing this, he was supposed to be heading for Milford Haven; he had become scared and was running for the land. Sometimes we

132

could not see a ship's length ahead, and still he kept running on, when all at once rocks were sighted quite close ahead. All hands were ordered up on the poop by the chief mate, as he stated that he would not be responsible for our lives any longer. The sea was terrific and was going right over the first rock sighted. More rocks were sighted, one of which we only cleared by about two cables' lengths. Later on when the squalls cleared away we saw the lighthouse; we were among the Smalls on the Welsh coast and not near Milford Haven.

The mate proved himself to be incompetent, and he was not justified in making for Milford Haven, especially as he did not know how the port bore. Apart from that, the ship was seaworthy and could have made a good stretch down Channel with the north-west wind. Nothing was seen of the captain during all this dangerous time. The second mate called him, but could not get him to understand that the ship was in a dangerous position.

After passing the Smalls, the mate hauled the ship more to the southward, the squalls cleared away and the weather became fine, although a heavy sea was still running. About seven o'clock we were off the Mumbles Head, near Swansea, when the mate decided to let go anchor. It was my trick at the wheel at the time. The mate gave me a course to steer; " Keep her that course," said he, " until I come back; I am going to get the anchors over the bows." He had scarcely left the poop, when the " Old Man " came up the companion-way, had a look all round, and then shouted out to me, " Luff you may."

I repeated the order after him, put the wheel down a few spokes, and then back again as soon as his back was turned. He was sober enough to notice that the ship was still heading in the same direction.

" Did I not tell you to luff? " he roared out.

" Luff it is, sir," I replied, and put the helm down as I was instructed.

This brought the sea on the starboard side, which made the ship roll the sea in over both sides. The anchors were now hanging by the ring stoppers, and with the heavy rolling they pounded against the ship's bows so heavily that they would have knocked holes in our bow-plates.

The mate came running aft to see what was the matter. " Did I not tell you," he said, " to keep the ship on the course I gave you until I returned to the poop? "

I explained to him that I was acting according to captain's orders.

" Hard up," he said, " put her on the course I gave you."

The captain, who was standing close by, remarked that it would be advisable to heave to on the starboard tack for the night.

The mate made no reply, but came and instructed me in an undertone to pay no attention to any order the captain gave me. The captain must have heard the instructions which the mate gave me ; he walked down the cabin stairs and was not seen on deck again for several weeks.

The ship was rounded to, off the Mumbles Head, and the port anchor was let go, with a long scope of chain paid out. No man but a fool would anchor a ship in such an exposed position. If the wind came away strong from anywhere between south and west the ship most decidedly would have been lost. The incapacity of the chief mate and the drunken state of the captain were criticised very severely by the most experienced men in the forecastle. Some of the men went so far as to suggest that we should refuse to go any farther in the ship, except a new captain be appointed to take command.

Next morning being fine, the chief mate decided to go ashore and telegraph to the owners of the ship that we had been obliged to put into Swansea Bay in distress. In fact, signals of distress which were hoisted when we began to shape a course for Milford Haven, were kept flying all day. The chief mate took four men out of his watch into the boat with him, and started off for Swansea about nine o'clock. He returned to the ship on the following day late in the afternoon.

The second mate had all hands engaged setting the rigging up, which was an easy matter with screw-rigging. The parrel of the main topsail yard was not broken, only the pins had worked out, and the whole after-part had dropped on deck. Everything aloft and on deck was ready for sea in three or four hours.

About seven o'clock that evening, Carmichael, the Glasgow man, made his secret known to all hands. He explained where all the whisky and beer were stowed, which meant taking the fore hatches off and getting at the beer for a start. He pointed out that the locking bars on the fore hatch could be easily sprung high enough in the middle to let the end of the bar slip out independent of the padlocks. As four men were ashore with the mate, there were only eight able seamen left on board. Gleeson the American, Armstrong from Barrow-in-Furness, and I, strongly objected; the other five men, however, decided that there was no harm in taking up a few bottles of beer after the hard time we had had outside, and besides, added Carmichael, the " Old Man " aft had been swilling it down good ever since we left Glasgow. What was sauce for the gander was sauce for the goose. One of the stowaways was told off to keep a lookout for the second mate, while the five men were trying to open up the fore hatch.

As Carmichael remarked, the locking bars were sprung up quite easily, the tarpaulins were pulled back, but owing to the ship being new the wooden hatch covers were a tight fit, and it took some time before one of them could be pulled off. After it came off it was all plain sailing, as Carmichael remarked when he led the way below among the cargo, followed by his brother, the Kelvinhaugh lad, and the small stowaway.

There was a small hatch in the forecastle which led into the chain locker, and there was also a small hatch between the chain locker and the forward 'tween deck. There was some cargo on the top of the latter hatch which prevented communication with the chain locker. When this cargo was shifted there was communication between the forecastle and the hold. In case of being taken by surprise, the fore hatch was put on and covered up again and the locking bars put on.

Carmichael, who was directing operations, was in great glee when the fore hatch was covered up again. " It is now all underground work," he remarked. He then went below among the cargo. He found a large amount of candles, and then the broaching of the cargo began in dead earnest. The beer was bottled and stowed in barrels holding about four dozen bottles in each. Carmichael gave orders to his assistants that one hundred bottles should be brought into the forecastle right off the reel, before a bottle was opened by anyone. Sacks full of bottles were dragged up through the chain locker into the forecastle, until the number must have reached nearly two hundred.

The drinking then started in earnest. As no corkscrews were available, the necks were broken off instead. In less than an hour Carmichael and his confederates were all drunk, and broken bottles were scattered all over the forecastle. All sailors, as a rule, want to sing when they get to the happy stage, but those men were dead drunk and sprawling over the forecastle floor too suddenly for any singing. It was a most disgusting sight to see men, made in God's image, brought below the level of animals, sprawling among broken bottles on a forecastle floor. The four Glasgow men were the worst, Carmichael especially. He was a man who lived for drink; he had no ambition in this wide world beyond drink. During the whole voyage he was planning how to get at the whisky in the after 'tween deck, when there was no access to the beer in the fore hold. As soon as Gleeson and I found out that he was planning ways and means of getting at the whisky we threatened to report him to the chief mate.

The following day was Sunday, and the men were dead to the world all day; as soon as they were able to drink they knocked the neck off another bottle and drank its contents. Old Slushy, the cook, came along and helped himself, and remained among the bottles. Things were getting so bad that I went aft and reported the matter to the second mate. All the remaining full bottles were picked up and put below to where they came from, and the small hatch between the chain locker and fore hold was nailed down securely. This put an end to the broaching of cargo for the time being.

The chief mate returned to the ship in the afternoon, and when he saw what had happened during his absence he was astonished, especially at the condition of the men and the amount of broken bottles lying about.

TROUBLE WITH THE CAPTAIN.

ON the following day (Monday) the weather was fine, with a light northerly breeze blowing. The chief mate decided to heave up anchor and proceed to sea. We started to heave in cable about nine, and it was nearly noon before we were under weigh. The five seamen would not turn out of their bunks; they said that they were too sick. The four stowaways refused also when they saw the men refuse. Gleeson the American got into a rage, and asked the mate how long he intended to allow those five men and four stowaways to lie loafing in their bunks while the rest of us were working our insides out.

"What can I do?" said the mate, "the men won't get out."

"Look here, Mister Second," said Gleeson to the second mate, "you are big enough to throw those fellows out of the forecastle, why don't you get busy? You know that it is not my place to go in and throw them out; I have to live among them."

The second mate replied that if it came to throwing drunk people out on deck, it would be better to start at the other end of the ship first (meaning the captain).

Shortly after this, when we were sheeting home the fore lower topsail, Gleeson rushed into the forecastle, where screaming began, and one stowaway after another was tumbled head foremost out on deck in good American style. They were led along to the forebraces, and the ropes were actually put into their hands. One who was not pulling felt the weight of Gleeson's boot. To use Gleeson's expression, he put the fear of God into them; he drove them before him all over the ship where there was pulling to be done. We had no steam in this vessel, everything had to be done by hand or by capstan, and although we had the four stowaways to help, it took us a long time to get the topsails mast-headed after we got under weigh.

As soon as the topsails were set we were sent to dinner, and about an hour afterwards the bos'n shouted out, "Loose and set the mainsail." On hearing this, Gleeson hauled Carmichael out of his bunk and ordered him out on deck to work. Carmichael objected to this kind of man-handling and showed fight. Gleeson caught him by the shoulder and dragged him out on deck, and the other four men were either chased out or dragged out in a similar manner. Gleeson had been second mate on American ships and was well accustomed to man-handling refractory men.

The weather still kept fine, and all sails were set except the royals. The wind remained north-west, and we had a fine run down Channel.

One thing none of us could understand, and that was why the chief mate carried the four stowaways back to sea again, or why he did not take them ashore with him to Swansea.

When we had been about four days at sea we experienced a strong blow from the south-west. We shipped a heavy sea which washed the whole watch away from the fore braces. One man by the name of Davidson was thrown up against the main fiferail and was rather badly hurt, so that he had to be carried into the saloon to be examined by the chief mate. He was put into a spare room right opposite to the captain's room.

On the following day, when the ship was rolling heavily, Davidson saw the captain coming out of the bathroom and making for his own room. The ship at the time gave a heavy roll to leeward and threw the captain up against the cabin stove with such force that he was knocked unconscious. Davidson, not being able to run to his assistance, shouted for the negro steward to come along and attend to the captain. The steward came along right away and laid the "Old Man" out on the carpet. He was still unconscious, and the blood was flowing profusely from a large wound above the right eye. The chief mate came along and dressed the wound, and with the assistance of the steward the "Old Man" was helped into his bed.

Davidson overheard a conversation between the chief mate and the steward. The steward informed the chief mate that the "Old Man" had drunk over a bottle and a half of whisky every day, and that there were only twelve or thirteen bottles left. The mate replied he had a good mind to take the remaining bottles of whisky from him and put him on a small allowance. The steward agreed to go into his room and bring them out, as he reckoned that he was almost on the verge of *delirium tremens*. The whisky was taken into the mate's room.

When the " Old Man " got out of his bed some hours later to have another drink he discovered that all his whisky was gone. He behaved like a madman. He roared out for the steward.

" Where is my whisky? " he yelled. " Steward, steward, where are you? Where is my whisky? "

" I am coming as soon as I get my clothes on," the steward called out.

The steward went to the captain's room and told him that the chief mate and he had considered it necessary to put him on an allowance of whisky.

" Bring the mate along at once," the " Old Man " called out.

The steward replied that the mate was asleep; it was his watch below.

The " Old Man " demanded his whisky at once. No man had a right to drink his whisky. He did not care a hang whether the mate was asleep or not.

The steward called the mate and told him that the captain wanted his whisky. The mate went along to the captain's room and asked what was the matter.

" Matter," roared the " Old Man." " Are you drinking my whisky, you thief of a poop ornament? You are no sailor, only a b——— ornament for strutting around a poop—that is telling you straight what you are. What right have you to come into my room and steal my whisky out of my spirit locker, you blarsted Scotch burgoo eater? "

" Look here, sir," said the mate, " I took your whisky away so as to keep you out of *delirium tremens*."

The " Old Man " threatened to show his authority as master of the ship. He would turn the mate into the forecastle. It lay in his power to either make or break him, and it was no affair of the mate's whether he (the " Old Man ") took *delirium tremens*, " stirricks," blue devils, or not. The mate, to avoid any further argument, went out on deck and left the " Old Man " swearing and using the foulest language which was ever inspired from Billingsgate.

The weather at this time was fairly fine again, the ship was going along steadily enough to allow the " Old Man " to leave his room, and on crossing the cabin he noticed Davidson in the spare cabin bunk.

" Who are you? " the " Old Man " demanded. " What in h— are you doing aft in my saloon? "

Davidson informed him that he had been hurt inwardly by a heavy sea that washed him away from the fore braces.

The " Old Man " ordered him out of the saloon at once, and called him for all the lazy, good-for-nothing sea-lawyers, who was only fit to eat hash and give impudence.

Davidson gathered himself together and made tracks for the forecastle, and as he went out through the front saloon door he turned round and had a parting shot at the " Old Man."

" You say, captain," said he, " I am only good for eating hash and giving impudence."

" Yes," said the captain, " that is all you are good for."

" I am for more use than you are, you drunken old swab," said Davidson, and with that he cleared away forward to the forecastle as fast as his injured condition would allow him.

The " Old Man " got on to the mate after this for having one of the crew comfortably stowed in a bunk in the spare cabin without his permission. Both men went into the saloon, and the man at the wheel could hear them quarrelling from where he stood. The chief mate must have stuck to his resolution in putting the " Old Man " on an allowance of whisky, as he managed to put in an appearance on the poop every day for a little while.

One day I was at the wheel when the " Old Man " came up on the poop. He came aft and had a look at the compass, looked aloft at the sails, and then at me.

" What course are you steering, my lad? " said he.

I replied, " South by west, three quarters west."

" Well, keep her that, and don't let her yaw about," said he. He walked fore and aft the poop a few times and had a look at the compass and sails again.   Turning round to me he said : " Keep the ship on her course, and don't be sculling her all over the ocean."

I replied that she was being kept very steadily on her course and had never been more than a quarter of a point off it.

" You are a liar," he shouted.   " You are more than a point off your course now."

" I am right on my course now," I replied.

He turned round and surveyed me with a malevolent look and shouted : " You are the young rascal who saw me defrauded out of thirty shillings by those thieves of riggers at the Gareloch anchorage."

I replied it was no affair of mine, and that I had nothing to do with it.

He turned round and shook his fist in my face, and told me that he would keep it off my wages and reduce me to ordinary seaman at a pound a month because I could not steer the ship properly.

I told him that I could steer the ship as well as any man on board and that he could not disrate me, for in addition to steering I was quite fit to perform the duties of an able seaman, and had served in that capacity quite a while before I came on that vessel.

He turned round, ground his teeth, clenched his fists, and glared at me with such a malignant look that I let go the wheel and faced him, ready to guard off any blow he might have made at me.

The wheel commenced spinning round and the ship came up in the wind and was laid flat aback.   The second mate came running up on the poop to see what was the matter, and was surprised to see the " Old Man " and me facing each other ready for a fight, and the wheel spinning round.

The first thing the second mate did was to put the wheel hard up and bawl out " Lee fore brace " to the men on deck.   The ship was running in the north-east trades, with the wind on the port quarter at the time.

" What is the matter, sir " the second mate enquired.

" Take and put this thief of a sea-lawyer in irons and feed him on bread and water," the " Old Man " roared out.

The chief mate, whose watch it was below, came running up

on the poop also. The second mate rushed down to fill on the fore yards, and I went back to the wheel.

"Mister," the "Old Man" shouted, "this is the rascal who was in league with the riggers at the Gareloch, who deliberately saw them defraud me out of thirty shillings, and when I came up on the poop I found him not steering the ship properly; he was steering west by south, three quarters south."

"No, no," the mate remarked, "that would be six points off her course, the sails would all be aback if that were the case."

"Can't you see for yourself, mister, that the ship is all aback," said the captain.

I informed the chief mate that the ship was steered properly, and that I had to let the wheel go in order to protect myself owing to the captain assuming an offensive attitude.

The "Old Man" called me a liar, and gave orders that I be sent away from the wheel at once, never to be allowed back again, and that I should be disrated to ordinary seaman. The chief mate sent word along to the second mate to relieve the wheel.

When I was walking forward along the lee side of the poop after being relieved, the "Old Man" turned round and asked me if I had been accustomed to walking along the weather side of the poop in ships that I had sailed in before. I must have given a derisive laugh at this remark, as the "Old Man" turned almost purple with rage. I pointed over to windward and said, "That is the weather side over there."

"In irons this bounder must go," the "Old Man" roared out, who was now beside himself with rage. "When you have him properly secured, mister, feed him on bread and water, a cupful of water and a biscuit twice a day, and three months in jail in Sydney on top of that. That is the way to fix you, my lad."

I walked down off the poop and took no more notice of him, as I came to the conclusion the man was mad. As it was my watch below at four o'clock, I managed to have a word with the chief mate after he came forward shortly afterwards. I explained how the trouble began, and that I had to let the wheel go in order to protect myself against what appeared to me to be a madman. The chief mate seemed satisfied with my explanation, and advised me to take no more notice of it.

The northern trade winds fell away very light, and we were becalmed for two full days in sight of the island of San Antonio, one of the Cape de Verd Islands. We could not have made more than twenty miles in the two days, and for that the southerly current would be responsible. The " Old Man " spent a while on the poop during the calm weather, and seemed to be improving both in mind and body. The bandages were removed from his head and his walk was much steadier. He did not seem to take any interest in navigating the ship, but left it to the chief mate to do.

We had quite a lot of doldrums around the equator and heavy rains, and in about three degrees south we ran into the south-east trade winds. I remained away from the wheel for about twenty days, when I was told to take my usual " trick " again.

When the " Old Man's " whisky gave out, his temper became worse than ever; he began interfering with everyone on board except the chief mate. He gave Old Slushy the cook a dressing down almost every day, especially on pea-soup days. The pea soup was either too thick or else too thin; the salt pork was either overboiled or underboiled. The second mate came in also for a dressing down sometimes, and very often within the men's hearing, which is against all reason.

Any captain who bullies his officers or speaks to them in a dis-respectful manner cannot expect good discipline to be maintained on board. If he has occasion to find fault with an officer it should be done in private and outside of anyone's hearing. A great many captains of sailing ships in those days were inclined to bully their officers in the presence of the men. This was chiefly owing to captains having too little exercise, which means a sluggish liver, and they came on deck in the morning with a bad taste in their mouths. Masters have the officers completely at their mercy. If a captain makes a bad report to his owners regarding an officer, that officer's prospects of promotion are very poor.

I was not the only man at the wheel who came in for the " Old Man's " bad temper. Davidson, the man who was injured through being washed away from the fore braces, came in for a fairly good share of the " Old Man's " displeasure. The " Old Man " never forgave him for calling him a drunken old swab.

One day the ship was caught aback in the doldrums when Davidson was at the wheel. The " Old Man " fairly raved. His bottled-up rage bubbled over as he stamped fore and aft the poop, stopping occasionally and shaking his fist in Davidson's face.

" Call yourself a sailor," he roared out. " You cannot steer, you thief of a sea-lawyer. I'll fix you, you loafer, you must be disrated to ordinary seaman."

Davidson, on hearing all this abuse, and knowing more about the captain's drinking than anyone else, lost his temper and told the captain to keep his fists away from his face. Davidson advised the " Old Man " to keep his temper as he (Davidson) was not going to be bullied by any drunken old tyrant, who was not fit to command any ship.

The " Old Man " shouted out to relieve the wheel at once. He was now choking with fury. Davidson was relieved in due course and was ordered down into the saloon to be disrated, logged and fined. The chief mate was brought into the saloon also as a witness. The official log was brought out and the chief mate was instructed to make the entry. The " Old Man " stated that the entry was to put on record that the man was incapable and unfit to fulfil the duties of an able seaman, and that his wages were to be one pound per month instead of three pounds per month. He was also to be fined for using insulting language to the commander of the ship, his fine to be one pound.

Davidson noticed that there were no entries in the official log, and made a remark to that effect.

" Captain," said he, " before you make any entry regarding me, make an entry about yourself, how you were drunk and incapable for three weeks."

On hearing this the " Old Man " made a rush at Davidson and caught him by the throat unawares. Both men fell on the saloon floor, the " Old Man " on the top with his fingers round Davidson's windpipe.

"Get your darbys (handcuffs) mister, while I hold the brute, quick!"

"You are strangling the man, captain," said the mate, "let him get up."

"I will choke the life out of him first," the "Old Man" hissed between his few stumps of rotten teeth.

The second mate, on hearing the scuffle, came along and assisted the mate in loosening the "Old Man's" hands from around Davidson's throat. Davidson, on being released, was past speaking; all he could do was to stand panting.

"This is mutiny on the high seas," the "Old Man" bellowed, "the whole three of you rascals will figure in the Newgate Calendar. I demand you to put that man in irons."

The two officers took no notice of him, but advised Davidson to clear away forward out of the way. What transpired after that between the captain and his two officers none of us ever knew. Davidson, however, was left alone for the rest of the voyage.

The "Old Man" put his temper out on Gleeson a few days afterwards. Gleeson was at the wheel, and the "Old Man" accused him of not answering in a civil manner. Gleeson told him that he was going mad and would be in the "bug house" before long. "Bug house" is an American term for a lunatic asylum. The "Old Man" raved and shook his fist in Gleeson's face for a while and then went below.

The negro steward and the "Old Man" became very friendly after this. The result was that he was not seen very much on deck, and when he did come he was "half-seas over," and to our relief never spoke to anyone. It soon became apparent to us that the steward was carrying rum to him from below. Sailing ships when starting on a voyage generally have a supply of rum on board, which is meant to be supplied to the crew in cases of emergency— such as shortening sail in stormy weather, or when extra work has to be done.

ANOTHER RAID ON THE CARGO.

THERE were others on board who had as great a thirst as the "Old Man" had, *viz.*, the "Glasgow push"—Carmichael and his brither (as he called him), Jock Farrell, the Kelvinhaugh lad, and the three other stowaways, one of whom was called Buffalo, another Dungannon, and Wee Sammie, who was a born crook and took a prominent part in broaching cargo when anchored off the Mumbles. The latter told his friends when he was drunk that he never did an honest day's work in his life, and he reckoned that he was somewhere about twenty years of age. He said that he found it necessary to stowaway as the police were getting down on him. When out of jail he generally lived in brothels. His friends of the "Glasgow push" called him Wee Sammie, and the rest of us always called him the "Pimp" and nothing else.

Although the sailormen of those days were rather rough men in some ways, they could not tolerate crooks of any kind. They were the most honest men living, and to their eternal sorrow they put implicit trust in all those crimps and harpies who lived on their hard-earned money.

The whole four stowaways seemed to belong to the underworld fraternity, and were treated as such by several of us. Although the officers were rather lax with them, we kept them up to the mark, and were not backward in giving them the "right about turn" when circumstances required it. Any hanging back or sour looks were soon thrashed out of them. Buffalo was a man about thirty, and considered that he had no right to be ordered about like a boy and do boy's work. In one particular instance he refused to clear the dishes away after meals. He went to bed instead, and was rewarded with a bucketful of water thrown over him and was then thrown head foremost out of the forecastle. Buffalo was kept out of the forecastle for two or three days until he promised faithfully to do what he was told.

The "Glasgow push" used to get away in corners to converse

by themselves, and when anyone passed them all conversation ceased. Carmichael and the " Pimp " (Wee Sammie) seemed to be the leaders in conversation, which made me very suspicious and gave me no end of anxiety, as I knew that Carmichael was planning how to get at the whisky and beer down in the hold. Carmichael and I were in the same watch, and I therefore made up my mind to watch him.

After we lost the south-east trade winds the weather became colder every day, and one night when we went off watch at midnight Carmichael remarked to me that he was going to warm up some cold tea on a slush lamp in the starboard lighthouse. I became suspicious, and about one o'clock I got up and looked into his bunk. He was not there. Dungannon and Wee Sammie were also away somewhere, which made me come to the conclusion that the fellows were up to some crooked business.

It was impossible to sleep, knowing that those men would most likely be broaching cargo in the hold in the vicinity of twenty tons of powder; knowing also that there were plenty of candles in the hold.

About three o'clock the whole three came slipping into the forecastle, which was quite dark (no lamp being lit). The next performance was pulling the cork out of a bottle with a corkscrew, and some whispering.

One man said: " Where did you get the corkscrew from, Sammie? "

Sammie replied that he stole it out of the pantry.

I could stand this no longer; up I jumped and held a lighted match in their faces. The rascals had been aft and probably near where the powder was stowed; they had five bottles of whisky standing beside them. A malignant look came over their faces when I shouted out, " Where have you been? Have you been down among the powder? "

All the other men jumped out of their bunks. One man shouted out, " Heavens, we are like men sitting on the top of a volcano ! " The three rascals sat thunderstruck at being surrounded by so many angry faces.

I picked up the five bottles (one of which had been broached).

"I am taking these bottles aft to the mate," said I, "to see if steps cannot be taken to prevent you whisky guzzlers from going into the ship's hold where twenty tons of high explosive powder is stowed."

Carmichael flared up at once and said that he had it from good authority that I was an informer—that when cargo was broached before I deliberately went and made the second mate wise on the fact.

"That is right," said I, "and I am going again; I don't want the ship to be blown up. Drunk men cannot be trusted with lighted candles among powder barrels."

It was still the mate's watch on deck when I took the bottles up on the poop to him. On seeing the bottles he was completely flabbergasted.

"Good heavens!" he said, "we may be blown to 'kingdom come' at any moment. Go and call the second mate at once; better call the carpenter, too."

After calling the second mate and carpenter, I went into the forecastle, where a real battle royal was going on. Carmichael was lying on the floor groaning and calling out, "Oh, my head; I am done for." Jock Farrell from Kelvinhaugh had come to the assistance of his townsman and had been promptly knocked out by Streeter, an Englishman. Gleeson had given the stowaways another thrashing. The mate came along with handcuffs, and we soon had the three rascals who had broached cargo handcuffed to the sparring in the sail locker, where they were kept for three days on a cup of water and a biscuit each per day.

In the forward deckhouse there was a trunkway about four feet square, extending from the skylight on the top of the house down into the top of the 'tween deck. This trunkway serves two purposes, viz., to ventilate the hold, and also, in a case of emergency, access can be had to the hold in bad weather when hatches cannot be opened. There were iron bars across to prevent people going down, such as in the case of broaching cargo. Those bars, however, are not heavy, and in our case Carmichael rigged a Spanish windlass and hove them closely together, and passed little Sammie down through into the hold.

As soon as this was discovered, the mate and carpenter went below with a Davy lamp and were able to find the whisky case that had been broached.   Several bottles had been taken out of the case.   The pillaged case was only five feet away from the powder magazine, and several matchpins were lying on the floor alongside of it.   No ship surely ever ran such a narrow escape of being blown up.   It appeared that no candle or light of any kind had been used, as there was a track of burned matches all the way from the trunkway to the pillaged whisky case.   The stowaway had crawled over the top of other cargo and had been lighting matches all the way.   A considerable amount of this cargo over which he had crawled was composed of silk goods and cloth, which could easily catch fire from lighted matches.   Many ships have disappeared on the voyage to Australia having a general cargo on board and a consignment of whisky amongst it.   The men were never brought before the captain, and whether he knew of it or not, none of us forward ever heard.   Every precaution was taken after this to make sure that there would be no access into the ship's hold.

A PERIOD OF GALES.

WE passed the island of Tristan da Cunha, in latitude 37° south and longitude 12° west, early on a Sunday morning. The island is high and can be seen about ninety miles off in clear weather. There were about eighty inhabitants on it about that time—half-breeds, descended from various races, chiefly from men who had run away from whalers which often used to call at the island. It is a British possession, and a Government vessel from the Cape Colony used to visit it about once a year. We passed it about eight or ten miles off, but did not have time to view it as all hands were engaged in shortening sail at the time. There are several smaller islands away to the southwards of it, uninhabited, one of which is called Inaccessible Island.

After passing Tristan da Cunha we had a howling gale behind us for two days, which took us into the "roaring forties." All that part of the Southern Ocean, viz., the southern part of the Atlantic, Indian, and Pacific Oceans, which lies between the latitudes of forty and fifty south, is called the "roaring forties." There one gale after another prevails at short intervals all the year round. Icebergs may be seen almost anywhere in these parts, chiefly in the summer time. As a rule the wind is westerly all the time, that is, between north-west and south-west. Our "Old Man" was scarcely ever seen on deck down in the "roaring forties." The working of the ship was left to the two officers, both of whom were very careful men, rather too careful sometimes, to our liking. When we were about on the meridian of the Cape of Good Hope and in about forty-four south, we experienced a terrific gale which started from the north-west and chopped to the south-west during a heavy squall. The wind and sea became so rough that the chief mate and second mate could not decide what to do—whether to run or heave-to.

The "Old Man" must have been drunk at the time, as this case was a matter for the commander to decide, after a consultation

150

with his officers.   Luckily two men were at the wheel, one of them being Gleeson the American, who was beyond doubt the most experienced man on board, and had been an officer in American ships for many years.   It is a most unusual thing for any officer to consult a man before the mast on any matter regarding the handling of a ship.   The mate, however, managed to get Gleeson's opinion in a somewhat round-about way, by remarking that "if the weather did not improve he would have to heave-to very soon before the sea became too rough."   Gleeson remarked that it was very risky heaving-to now as the sea was too heavy, and that serious damage would be done.

The mate decided to run under two lower topsails, reefed foresail, and fore topmast staysail.   The gale still increased and heavy seas tumbled on board; the decks were full up fore and aft, with only the tops of the deckhouses in sight sometimes.   The wind backed to the west and blew harder than ever, the starboard fore sheet carried away and the sail went to pieces.   In a few seconds there was nothing left except the bolt ropes.   The ship ran drier after this sail was blown away.   At two o'clock in the morning we could not see a ship's length ahead; the rain came down in torrents, and balls of fire could be seen at each yardarm and at sheave holes at the mastheads.

At four o'clock in the morning, whilst a young Scotsman was trying to get aft to relieve the wheel, we shipped a very heavy sea which swept him overboard, and he was seen no more.   Nothing could be done for him, as no one saw him being washed overboard; and even if anyone had seen him, nothing could have been done in such a dark, stormy night.   When a man loses his life so suddenly on board a ship it throws a gloom fore and aft, especially amongst those who come in daily contact with him.   Sudden death at all times is solemn, especially at sea, where twenty-five to thirty men are cooped up in a vessel for three or four months and see no faces but their own.   The empty bunk in the forecastle is there to remind them that one of their number has gone to a sailor's grave.   There would be one man less to haul, reef, or steer, down in the "roaring forties."   As is usual on board a sailing ship when a sudden death takes place, everyone has something to relate regarding the good qualities of the deceased. One would say that Joe was a good shipmate and sailorman. Another would say, " Poor Joe has gone on his last cruise; he is better off today than we are," etc.

The weather gradually moderated after this, and by noon we were under plain sail again. The heavy seas had bent in the starboard bulwark nearly a foot at the widest part, lamp room and paint locker were gutted out, and the water was washing into the lower bunks in the apprentices' quarters.

" Jumbo," the fat apprentice, reckoned that he was about four stones lighter since he joined in Glasgow. He showed us how he had taken in his belt seven holes, and his waistcoat could almost go twice round him. He was now able to go up and loose a royal. Owing to his being always hungry, he used to prowl around the steward's pantry and do odd jobs for the steward, who gave him whatever was left over from the cabin meals.

" Jumbo " showed me his kit one day, which, he said, cost his father £84. There used to be outfitters in London who specialised in sea apprentices' outfits, some of whom were very honest, and proper people to go to, but there were others who palmed off all kinds of rubbish on boys whose parents had no idea what a sea apprentice needed. " Jumbo " and his father had fallen into the hands of the latter kind of outfitter. His sea-chest was a large black-painted box like a packing case, not dove-tailed but knocked together any way. There were small racks for holding odds and ends, such as half a dozen egg cups, pepper dish, tooth brushes, shaving brushes, two table spoons, two dessert spoons, two tea spoons, two forks and knives, a cheap spyglass, and a whole lot of other useless trash to run up a bill. A fork and knife and a spoon would be about all he could find use for.

During the cold weather in the " roaring forties," or off Cape Horn, it is usual to give seamen oatmeal porridge and molasses for breakfast, owing to the heating tendency it has in cold weather. We had been on our bare allowance of food ever since we came on board, and had often asked the negro steward when porridge was to be served out. He replied that he had no authority to serve it out, and that we had better see the " Old Man " about it.

After the gale the " Old Man " came out, and three of us went along to see him. He was standing gazing at some albatrosses, and as soon as he heard us behind him he wheeled round and demanded to know what we wanted on his poop. We replied that we had come to see him about getting some burgoo, as it was customary in all deep-water ships to serve it out in cold weather.

" Oh," said he, " you want burgoo, do you? You are not going to get any. You get your whack of food, and you get no more, savvy? "

We replied that the oatmeal was put on board for that purpose, and that we had a right to it.

On hearing this, he went into a passion and roared out, " Get down off my poop, you cheeky lot of sea-lawyers, or else I'll have the whole three of you in irons before you know where you are."

Gleeson, the American, replied : " Nothing doing, captain, in the way of irons or handcuffs, they are out of season just now, just like your whisky, which is all done; and now you are washing down our rum which was put on board for us."

On hearing this, the " Old Man " went almost purple with rage. " You cheeky Yankee thief of a sea-lawyer, what business is it of yours whether I drink whisky or rum? I am my own master, and king of this island, I will have you to understand. How dare you come up on my poop and insult me, and demand whatever food you want."

We tried to reason with him, and after a little he calmed down and sent for the steward. The steward informed him that there was a barrel of oatmeal on board.

" We will need that for poultices," the " Old Man " replied.

The steward informed him that there was the usual Board of Trade supply of linseed meal on board, which would probably be sufficient to meet any requirements.

" How comes it about that the Board of Trade supply linseed meal? "

K

"They do not supply it," the steward said, "they demand that the ship should carry a certain amount at the owners' expense."

"Well," said the "Old Man" to the steward, "let them have as much burgoo as they want."

A HECTIC TIME IN SYDNEY.

WHEN we were in about 44° south and 84° east we sighted a huge iceberg at midnight and only cleared it by a few ships' lengths. The weather was thick at the time but not thick enough to prevent our seeing the berg much earlier. A bad look-out must have been kept by the second mate and the man on the look-out. To give the second mate credit, he showed good presence of mind in keeping the ship clear of it, and as soon as he saw it he sent an apprentice to call the " Old Man."

The apprentice returned to the poop and reported that he could not make the " Old Man " understand what he meant; all he could get out of him was a grunt.

It has been a recognised fact that officers of sailing ships kept a good look-out to windward, but not to leeward. They used to walk fore and aft along the weather side of the poop and scarcely ever went to leeward, where the danger generally lay. It is a fairly easy matter keeping clear of vessels or obstructions to windward, but it is a very different matter clearing anything to leeward.

We ran up against a small berg, which we only touched slightly. The pump-well was sounded occasionally and found to be quite dry.

After this, fine weather was experienced all the way to the Australian coast. We passed south of Tasmania without sighting anything, and the first land we made was that around Jervis Bay, about four o'clock in the afternoon.

The " Old Man " came up to see the land—the first time we had seen him for about three weeks. He had no idea where we were, and even when the second mate told him it was Jervis Bay he asked how far it was from Sydney Heads. No one could help despising a captain of this kind—a rum-soaked old fool who was not fit to command anything on the High Seas. He must have passed his examinations at the time when candidates worked their problems out on slates.   He told the second mate that he had never been to Australia before.

The wind was fresh and we were off Sydney Heads at two o'clock next morning.   We hove to, and commenced burning blue lights for a pilot.   We were then away about eight miles south-west from the South Head Lighthouse.   The " Old Man " came up and wanted to stand out to sea until daylight.   The mate stated that we would find ourselves to leeward of the Heads and would not be able to make them, which would mean a heavy towage bill.

The " Old Man " went below, and the mate took the opportunity during his absence of heading in towards the South Head, and hove to, awaiting the pilot.   When the " Old Man " came up on the poop again he gave orders to stand out to sea.   The mate tried to persuade him that the ship was in a good position for getting a pilot, but the " Old Man " was adamant, and shouted out, " We'll be ashore in a few minutes, mister ; we are close up to the rocks now.   Are you responsible for the ship or am I, mister? "

" Here's the pilot coming out, sir," the mate called out from the front of the poop.   The pilot came on board, and a tug showed up a few minutes later.

The tug came alongside and offered to tow us in for £25.   The " Old Man " offered £15.   " No good," the skipper of the tug replied.

The " Old Man " turned round on the mate and remarked, " This is a fine how do you do, mister.   We are in among the rocks and the skipper of the tug is taking advantage of it."

The pilot then spoke up and said that we were nearly five miles off the Heads, and that the charge was quite reasonable.   I was at the wheel at the time and noticed how the pilot was scrutinising the " Old Man," who looked at the time more like a rag-gatherer than the master of a fine new ship on her first voyage.   He had an old brown tam-o'-shanter on his head, and a coat with very short tails, a huge muffler two turns round his neck, and a pair of thick sailor mittens on his hands.   After a great deal of persuasion the " Old Man " agreed to take the tug for £24—the towboat skipper reduced his price one pound, and not a penny more would be come down.

Our towline passed on board the tug, we headed for the harbour entrance and anchored in Watson's Bay a little before daybreak.   After receiving pratique at sunrise, we hove up anchor and towed to the powder ground to discharge our twenty tons of explosives.   When heaving up anchor at Watson's Bay there was a considerable amount of chanteying done which irritated the " Old Man " considerably.   The first chantey was " Leave her, Johnny, leave her " :

> "A leaky ship and a drunken skipper,
> It is time for us to leave her;
> Captain drinks whisky and rum,
> Leave her, Johnny, leave her;
> Captain drinks whisky and rum,
> It is time for us to leave her," etc.

The " Old Man " must have been a coasting man and unaccustomed to hearing chanties, as he roared out from the poop to the chief mate to stop that song.   The mate took no notice, but remarked to the men as they walked round the capstan, " You men hear what the captain says."   No notice was taken, and " Leave her, Johnny, leave her " was increased in length.

After getting rid of our powder we started unbending sails. The captain went ashore when we started this work and did not return until the evening of the following day, when we were moored in our discharging berth at Millar's Point.   Everyone was tired of sailing with a drunken captain, so we all decided on going aft and demanding to be paid off.   We requested the steward to inform the captain that all hands wished to see him.   On seeing us all standing before him he demanded to know what our business was.   Gleeson, the American, being the oldest and most experienced man, informed him that we were tired of him, and wished to sail no longer with him owing to his intemperate habits.   On hearing this, he got into a terrible rage and, pointing to the wharf, he roared out, " If you do not like me or my intemperate habits, as you call it, there is the wharf, 'oof it, you scums of creation.   I don't want you here.   Get, before I send for a policeman."

It was no use trying to reason with him, so all hands marched forward again and held a council of war.   The majority favoured going ashore and reporting the captain's conduct to a magistrate.

I was in the minority, and wanted to wait and see how the " Old Man " behaved himself in port. Next morning four men went ashore to make arrangements with a lawyer to bring the " Old Man " to answer to the charge of drunkenness on the High Seas and endangering the lives and limbs of his crew.

The " Old Man " was on the poop and saw the four men going on shore with their best clothes on. On seeing them he ordered them back to the ship. The men took no notice of him, but walked on, followed by the " Old Man " who, when near the police station in George Street, gave them in charge for being ashore without leave. The men were locked up right away, and had to appear at the Water Police Court, where they received forty-eight hours' imprisonment for being ashore without leave.

The mate ordered the four stowaways on shore as soon as the ship arrived alongside her discharging berth, and informed them that if they ever showed their faces on board again they would be arrested and get six weeks for stowing away on board the vessel. The night watchman, who was an elderly man by the name of Jacob, a Swede, was instructed not to let them on board during the night.

They did not show up the first night, but on the second night three of them sneaked on board, and when all was quiet, Carmichael the sailor, and his brother, and the other two stowaways managed to get into the hold through a large ventilator. Wee Sammie, the little stowaway, was passed down and started broaching cargo again. Six cases of whisky were opened up, and the bottles were passed ashore to some accomplices who were on the wharf according to arrangement. Cases containing silken goods were also broken into and their contents were hauled up on deck. Old Jacob, the night watchman, who had been ashore all afternoon was well under the influence of liquor when he went on duty, and during the time that the cargo was being broached he must have been asleep. All the afterguards were ashore, and although two men were in the forecastle the broaching of cargo passed unnoticed by them.

On the following day Carmichael and Jock Farrell, the Kelvin-haugh lad, were scrubbing the ship's side next to the wharf.

Instead of using stages, they used a small punt which they could reeve out and in among the piles. Jock Farrell had been up to the forecastle for a smoke, and seeing a chance of getting into the hold, he jumped down the fore hatch, walked aft along the 'tween deck, and collared a case of whisky. This he carried forward, and when he saw a suitable chance passed it over the side to Carmichael, his mate.

The two men drew their punt about twenty feet under the wharf and hid all the whisky except a bottle for present use. It was not long before they began to make merry, which drew the second mate's attention. On sliding down the ship's side over a rope he noticed an empty whisky bottle floating in the water, and the two men engaged in getting another bottle out of a bag; he also noticed the empty whisky case floating in the water. On seeing this, he ordered the men up on deck at once.

Carmichael used an offensive epithet towards the second mate, and added that they would come on deck in their own good time. The second mate went away until such time as the two rascals came up on deck. Jock Farrell climbed up and sent a rope down for the bag containing the whisky bottles, which they took into the forecastle.

The second mate followed them, and was apparently talking to Jock Farrell, who was the soberer, when Carmichael got behind him somehow and upset him. Both men now got on to him, and had it not been that the carpenter came along and ran to his assistance he would never have been able to get up off the floor. Carmichael was in the act of striking him on the head with a heavy boot-jack when the carpenter grabbed it. As soon as the second mate got up there was a rough house for a few minutes.

The fight was cut short by the arrival on the scene of the chief mate and two policemen, who assisted the second mate. Both men were clapped in irons and dragged out of the forecastle. They sat down on the deck and would not get up; the baton was used on them freely.

The second mate had to assist the policemen in getting them over the gangway, and when they reached the wharf they presented a pitiful appearance. They were bare to the waist owing to their upper clothing being torn off their bodies, barefooted, and their faces all covered with blood. They were taken all the way to the police station in George Street. When they were being taken up the wharf they were singing "We will roll the old chariot along."

Their case came up at the Water Police Court on the following day, and each received twelve weeks' imprisonment.

Owing to so much cargo having been pilfered, the agents of the ship engaged detectives to go into the matter. Wee Sammie had been camping on the domain along with Carmichael's brother and another stowaway, where all three were arrested. They had been going around several small drapers' shops with silken goods for sale; and the liquor had been taken and sold to a low-down pub., upon the rocks above the Argyle Cut, called the "Black Dog." Quite a lot of the stolen property could not be traced, and the detectives came to the conclusion that the longshoremen had been taking a large amount also. Two apprentices were stationed in the hold to see that the cargo was not pilfered, but owing to the ship being badly disciplined, the boys were as careless as the rest of the crew. The three stowaways were also sentenced to twelve weeks' imprisonment.

When the four men who went ashore to bring a charge against the captain for drunkenness on the High Seas came out of prison, they came across a shady lawyer who undertook to take up their case. In due course the captain was summoned to appear at the Water Police Court, and nearly all the crew were summoned also to appear as witnesses.

The men's lawyer at the beginning of the trial called the judge's attention to the fact that the captain was then nearly drunk, which spoke for itself. "No man," said he, "shows his hand before he starts playing a game at cards." Several witnesses were called, and none could actually swear that they saw the captain drunk and incapable.

The captain's lawyer maintained that before a man could be called drunk he must be incapable, unfit to stand up, and yet not a witness could swear that he saw the captain even stagger. Regarding the captain not being on duty when the ship was nearly lost on the Smalls, that could be easily explained, as the captain caught a chill leaving Glasgow, and was unfit to come on deck. The whole business was fishy, he said. " Here were a lot of unscrupulous men trying to victimise their captain for their own personal gain, namely, to get paid off in full, and then get higher wages in another ship." The captain's lawyer also commented on the remark made by the men's lawyer regarding the captain being under the influence of liquor. " The captain," he said, " was so terribly worried and upset through this trouble with his men that he was bordering on a nervous breakdown."

The judge dismissed the case, and all hands were ordered on board by the captain, who stated that those who were not at work on the following morning would be arrested and imprisoned.

Next morning at 6 o'clock the second mate came along and shouted out, " All hands muster on the quarter-deck." The " Old Man " was standing there, whilst the chief mate called our names out. The muster was a small one.

" Three men short," the mate remarked to the captain. " Where is Larsen? " the mate asked us.

Davidson from Dundee replied, " Larsen 'as 'oofed it."

" Where is Gleeson? "

" Gleeson 'as 'oofed it, and Phillips also 'as 'oofed it."

We all started laughing, and yet the " Old Man " did not seem to understand what we were laughing at, which showed how illiterate he was.

The " Old Man " now started on to us. " You bloomink lot of b——s," said he, " I'll 'ave no more of your bloomink shinnanigin, you mawk my words. I am going to make yer all clawr the dust; yer thought that yer 'ad me, did yer? He larfs longest who larfs last. I 'ave a surprise pawket up my sleeve yet; you watch me." He stood cursing and threatening us for over a quarter of an hour, and none of us took any notice of him.

Old Jacob Larsen, the night watchman, had deserted, and I was told off to keep night watch.

One fine Saturday night about ten o'clock the second mate came on board after having had a few drinks. He became very confidential and informed me that the " Old Man " had got into trouble at the Mercantile Marine Office over the official log. The superintendent had threatened to report the matter to the Board of Trade. The log contained no entry regarding the man getting his leg broken in the Irish Channel, no entry regarding the draft of water leaving Glasgow or on leaving the Tail of the Bank. No entry regarding putting in and anchoring off the Mumbles, and finally no entry regarding the loss of the man overboard. The " Old Man " apparently did not understand how to make those entries, and asked the second mate to help him.

That same night the chief mate came on board and discovered that the negro steward had two lady friends in his room. He promptly ordered them on shore, adding that no respectable woman could be on board a strange ship at that time of night. The steward became so annoyed at this remark that he threatened to break every bone in the mate's body. The mate made no remark, but walked ashore and returned in about a quarter of an hour's time with two policemen to arrest the steward. At the police court on Monday the steward was sentenced to seven days' imprisonment.

During the time I was keeping night watch the " Old Man " generally came on board about three in the morning, and twice he asked me in a sarcastic manner if I considered he was sober.

The second time that he asked me I replied that whether he was drunk or sober it was no affair of mine; and further, that although I was summoned to court as a witness I had nothing to do with any conspiracy against him; and also, the evidence given by me did not reflect anything to his discredit.

He turned round and told me that he admitted that my evidence given in court did not hurt him in the least, but still he had not forgotten the fact that I could have saved him the thirty shillings he overpaid the riggers at the Gareloch.

I then asked him if he would pay me off, as I did not wish to remain any longer in the ship. His answer was that he would not, and that he was not finished with me yet.

A TRIP UP COUNTRY AND BACK IN SYDNEY.

ON the following day news came that as soon as the cargo was out the vessel was to load coal for Guayaquil in Ecuador, which was one of the worst places in the whole world for yellow fever.

All hands but four had now deserted, and as soon as we heard this news the rest of us decided to desert too. My time was about up for sitting for my second mate's examination, and if I deserted I could not go up for another two years. After studying the situation from all points of view, I made up my mind to clear out. The captain was not a fit man to sail with; he was totally unfit to command any kind of vessel, and if I remained in the ship he would refuse to give me a recommendation, and probably would give me a bad discharge. At that time every candidate going up for a Board of Trade examination had to have a testimonial for his last twelve months' sea service.

As the vessel was going to Guayaquil, this, also, to a certain extent, influenced me. If the captain had been a fairly decent man and the ship all right, I would not have deserted. By taking this step I forfeited all the wages due me, which amounted to £11. That gave me no concern, as I had a few pounds which I brought on board with me.

The bos'n, a Norwegian, had had no trouble with the captain or officers, yet on the night on which we deserted he cut a considerable amount of the running gear and threw the cat blocks for catting the anchors, and the capstan bars, into the harbour. When we found out what he had done we all got on to him and let him know what we thought of him. We told him that most likely we would all be arrested over his spiteful disposition, and if such should happen we would most certainly not suffer for his dirty work.

This is where the Britisher differs from the foreigner. When a Britisher is not satisfied with his ship and deserts at some port

163

abroad, he leaves her with clean hands; the foreigner, on the other hand, is spiteful, and would sink the ship if he possibly could.

I remember being in Freemantle anchorage in command of a sailing ship in 1897 when two of my men deserted. They slipped over the stern and took the ship's gig to row ashore in. When they reached the jetty they tied the boat's painter to a ring where she could lie in safety : those two men were Britishers. Four men belonging to another ship deserted that same night, and as soon as they reached the shore they smashed the boat up before leaving it. Three of those men were Dutchmen or Germans, and the other a Belgian.

When we deserted our vessel we took steamer to Newcastle, which is 60 miles north of Sydney, and when we landed we went to the Sailors' Home and left our belongings there—all except enough clothing to make up a swag. We decided it would be advisable to get up country in case a warrant had been issued for our arrest. It was on a Saturday afternoon when we started up-country with our swags on our shoulders.

To make up a swag you lay a blanket on the ground, put a shift of clothes inside, and roll it up neatly. When rolled up it is about two feet long ; two leather straps go round it, and a third strap goes over your shoulder.

When we were about six miles out of Newcastle we came across a gang of men who were making a road through the bush. The ganger offered us a job at felling trees, or wheelbarrow work. There was a plank about twenty feet long, a foot wide, and three inches thick, stretched across a gully about eight feet deep at the deepest part. I was the first volunteer for the wheelbarrow, and managed fairly well although the plank was springy. The ganger was quite satisfied. The next man was Davidson, from Dundee, who started off with his loaded barrow, and when he was nearing the middle where the gully was deepest, the wheelbarrow and all went off the plank into the gully. The ganger told him to try the empty barrow first. Davidson tried the empty barrow, which he managed to steer to the other side although twice it nearly went over. We tried tree-felling, which greatly amused the practical men and disgusted us.

We thanked the ganger and went on our journey towards a railway station called Tara, where we intended to take train for a place several miles up the line.   We reached Tara station sometime about midnight, and slept in the waiting-room until five o'clock next morning, when the station-master called us and told us that the distance to our destination was only about eight miles or so, and suggested that we should take the road and not wait on the train. We started off, and about nine o'clock we came to a hut where a woman stood at the door.   We asked her if she could give us breakfast, saying we would pay her for it.   She invited us in, and before long we were served with tea, bread and butter, and three mutton chops apiece.   We paid her for our meals and started off in the direction she pointed out to us.

All went well until we came to the junction of two roads, where, unfortunately, we took the wrong turn, and before long we found ourselves in the heart of a dense forest.   Towards noon the heat was oppressive and the mosquitoes were out in millions. Snakes were also very numerous, and when we sat down to rest on a log a huge snake almost pounced on Davidson.   It must have been nearly six feet long.   It was a tiger snake, one of the most ferocious and venomous snakes in Australia with the exception of the death adder.   The latter is the most dangerous reptile in Australia, and death sometimes takes place a few minutes after being bitten.   It is very sluggish in its habits, until trodden on, when it strikes right away.   The tiger snake gets its name from its stripes across its body.

We must have been wandering about for some four hours before we came to open country.   We saw a farmhouse in the distance and made for it.   As we were terribly dry, we asked the farmer for a drink of water.

" Sure," said the farmer, " and its not water yez are wanting, it's milk yez are wanting and milk yez are going to get."

The farmer went in and brought us a large billy full of milk and a two-pound loaf.   " I take it," said he, " that yez are runaway sailors from some ship."

We admitted that we were, and we hoped that he would not give us away to the police.

" It's tongue-tied I'll be if any peeler comes here asking for yez, for sure I have been at say mysilf for foive years, and like yez I ran away too.   I ran from the Red Jacket in Melbourne twenty years or more ago."   He told us that he came from County Wexford in Ireland, and had to work as a farm-hand for quite a while before he was able to have a place of his own.   He gave us to understand that he was well off and had nearly 200 acres of good land, and milked a large number of cows.

Bidding good-bye to our Irish friend we started off on the tramp again, and came to a place called Miller's Forest.   As we passed a very neat-looking farmhouse the farmer came out and asked if we were runaway sailors and where were we making for. We admitted that we were runaways and were making for a place near Morpeth.

" You had better not go there," said the farmer.   " You will be going right into the dog's mouth if you go there, owing to several troopers and black trackers being stationed there."   He suggested that one of us should stay with him as he was needing some help.

Taylor agreed to remain with the farmer, and Davidson and I bade him good-bye and made tracks for a township called Raymond Terrace.   There was a policeman there who seemed to take no notice of us, which made us come to the conclusion that there was no warrant out for our arrest.

Raymond Terrace is a small township on the banks of the Hunter River and is somewhere about fifteen miles away from Newcastle.   We obtained fairly good lodgings, and we were offered a job straight away to do some rigging work, and bend the sails on a fairly large barquentine hailing from Rockhampton. There was no one standing by her but the captain.

After our job was completed the captain found that he would not need us for a few days, and we took passage in the river steamer down to Newcastle to get a permit to ship in the barquentine.   On arrival we went to the shipping master, who, however, refused to give us permits until the ship we deserted left Australia.   This debarred us from going on the barquentine or any other British vessel until our late vessel sailed for Ecuador.   We went to the

Sailors' Home, where our effects were stored, to wait until the vessel sailed.

That same afternoon, to our surprise, we saw the vessel towing into the Horse Shoe—the ship we had deserted following us up. We all understood that she was to load coal in Sydney, and here she was.   Davidson and I came to the conclusion we had better take the steamer that night again back to Sydney.   We settled up at the Sailors' Home and left Newcastle by the 11 o'clock boat for Sydney, where we arrived the following morning at six o'clock and went to the Sydney Sailors' Home.   Here, again, the shipping master informed us that he could not give us a permit until our ship left Newcastle.

When walking along Pitt Street on the second day we were in Sydney we spotted our " Old Man " in the distance, coming directly towards us accompanied by a German doctor whom we had seen on board when we were discharging our powder into the powder hulk.   The " Old Man " seemed very agitated, and was talking about the mate and second mate, and never seemed to take notice of us.

The German doctor was brought on board to Neilsen, a Norwegian, who had been laid up for several days prior to our arrival at Sydney.   The man stated that he had consumption and was unable to work.   The German doctor examined him and stated that he had a pair of lungs as strong as a donkey boiler. Neilsen was " working the point " to get paid off, but, after the doctor's report, there was nothing doing.

We met several of the crew who were still unemployed, being, like ourselves, unable to get a ship while our last ship was still in Australian waters.   Gleeson was staying in the Sailors' Home and working on board a large American ship hailing from Richmond, Virginia.   He informed me that our old captain had been " fired " (as he called it), and the chief mate had been put in command. The agents had reported the captain's bad conduct to the owners of the ship, who had cabled to dismiss him.   He was staying in some low-down hotel in Upper George Street, and, according to Gleeson's version, he would soon be on the after-leeches of his shoes and sleeping on the domain.   The domain is a large tract of ground where all the hard-ups sleep. It lies between Sydney and Woolloomoolloo, and is quite handy to either place.

Gleeson informed me that several of the crew were sleeping on the domain, also the two apprentices, " Jumbo " and Clark—both having deserted their ship. I was sorry to hear this, and made it my business to go to the domain and try and find the two boys. The domain is a large place. I had to walk almost all over it, when I came across Jacob, the Swede, who was too drunk to get much sense from. He had not seen the boys that day, but reckoned that I might be able to find them in the Botanic Gardens which adjoined the domain.

I had not quite reached the gate when I met the two boys. They had a down-and-out look about them. " Jumbo " was as thin as a crane, and Clarke, the clergyman's son, seemed to have deteriorated considerably since I last saw him. His face and hands were dirty, and his clothes were covered with grass and clay : he seemed to have lost all self-respect. They told me that on the night they left the ship they sold all their clothes except what they stood up in—uniform suits also, in order to buy food. They tried to get work but failed to get any ; wherever they went they were laughed at. This money they handed over to an old lady who kept a small eating-house in George Street, so they did not starve. They knew that the captain had been dismissed from the ship and that the chief mate was in command.

I advised them to write to the new captain and explain to him that they left the ship owing to the late captain being a drunkard, and that they were prepared to return to the ship again. Clarke would not agree to this suggestion, but " Jumbo " considered that it was the right thing to do. I offered to write and explain how the boys were situated, that they were without clothes, and very soon would be without money.

Clarke was an obstinate lad and would not think of returning to the ship again. The sea, he said, was not for him ; the discipline on board ship was intolerable. It was " boy this " and " boy that," " boy, light the binnacle," etc. The sea, he said, had nothing to recommend it. His people at home would be sitting in a large carpeted drawing-room before a large fire, while he had to sit in the half-deck shivering during his watch below, without any fire and about a foot depth of salt water over the floor. His people at home closed the doors on a cold stormy night to keep the bad weather out, whilst at sea one had to close oneself out and either get washed about the decks like a cork or else washed over the side.

I tried to explain to him that the best that he could do was to go back to the ship, and if he had not changed his mind on arrival home, he could then leave and be among his own people. I also pointed out to him that Great Britain owed her prosperity to her seamen, and that it would be a sorry day for her if all her young men were like him. He then raised the point about the ship going to a sickly port, and that he did not wish to leave his bones in a place like Guayaquil. I promised to call and see them again about nine o'clock that evening, just to see how the down-and-outs put up for the night.

I met the boys at nine, as arranged. There was a tall, thin, sallow-looking man sitting beside them under a tree, whom they introduced as the doctor of the domain. He rose to his feet and gave me a hearty welcome.

" I am always glad," said he, " to meet a seafaring man as I have been at sea myself. I am sorry that my friend, Captain Gibson, is not here at present, as he would also be glad to see you. These two lads, Captain Gibson and I, claim this tree as ours. This is tree number eleven of Jackson Row. This is our kitchen, dining-room, drawing-room and bedroom, all rolled into one."

A few minutes afterwards two of the occupants of the next tree came along. One was an Irishman with a large nose, whom the others called Daniel O'Conner, the dismal Jimmy of Jackson Row. The other man was called the professor, who was to give a lecture on Darwinism. The doctor, however, reckoned that the professor had been partaking a little too freely of stimulants that evening to follow up the thread of his discourse. The professor denied that, and stated that he never was in a fitter condition to lecture on this particular subject since his 'varsity days.

I paid very little attention to the lecture—all that I remember was that the professor pointed out to us that if any animal—

L

whether human being, bird of the air, fish in the sea—in short, any living thing, desired to alter its appearance for reasons of its own, it would, in a few generations, have its wishes accomplished. For instance, the Polar bear, perhaps thousands of years ago was brown or black, and when he migrated to the Polar Regions he saw that a white coat was necessary to evade the keen eyes of the hunter. It was also necessary to be the same colour as the snow when he was out hunting on his own. All living things desired to change their colour to the same as their surroundings.

Daniel O'Conner was starting to give a lecture on the immortality of the soul, when I begged to be excused as I had some distance to go.

The two boys informed me afterwards that the doctor was a medical man at one time and had sailed as a surgeon on the Orient Line of steamers, but drink had put him under, and all he had to live on was his remittance of £3 per week from relations in England. The professor was also a remittance man. He, however, earned some money as a waiter and at other odd jobs around hotels. Daniel O'Conner was considered by some to be a broken-down priest, and did odd jobs on the racecourse and around hotel kitchens. He was also what was called a " spouter " on the domain on Sundays. His subject generally was on downtrodden Ireland. Captain Gibson was an ex-captain in the Army, also a remittance man, and an amateur boxer, who spent a lot of his time with Larry Foley, a professional boxer.

In the fine season hundreds of men slept on the domain, which in those days was a paradise for down-and-outs, loafers, beach-combers, remittance men belonging to good families, and bushmen from up-country who had come down to the city to knock their cheque down and have a roaring good time. The police, as a rule, never troubled the domain fraternity except when they were looking for someone. Hobos from the United States often found their way to Australia, and finally slept on the domain. Many respectable tradesmen have been reduced in circumstances and obliged to sleep on the domain.

I made another call on the two apprentices and managed to persuade them to come with me to see the superintendent of the

Mercantile Marine office on the following day. I explained to him that the boys were destitute, had sold all their clothing to buy food, and soon would be on the verge of starvation. The superintendent—an ex-sea captain—advised them to go back to their ship at once—that very night—and requested me to go and see them off in the Newcastle boat. I went up with them to the domain as they wished to say good-bye to their friends before leaving. The professor and Daniel O'Conner were in a drunken sleep, but the doctor was quite sober, and, on parting with the boys, he gave them good advice, and held himself up as an example. He called himself a drunken derelict; if it had not been for drink he could have risen to the top rung of the ladder of the medical profession.

I saw the two boys off in the Newcastle boat, and received a letter from them two days afterwards stating that the new captain (former chief officer) treated them very kindly, and had promised to give them a rig-out of clothes.

ON AN AMERICAN SHIP.

THAT same day I started work on the American ship Charles Dennis—the same ship that Gleeson was working on. She was discharging only part of her cargo at Sydney and was going round to Melbourne with the remainder. She had come from Puget Sound with timber, and had rough weather on the Australian coast before her arrival in Sydney. The crew had deserted as soon as she arrived in Sydney, and the captain wanted men to do some rigging work. She had lost her fore topgallant mast and jib-boom. The remains of the broken spars had to come down and the new ones rigged in their places. There were five of us engaged at five shillings per day and our food.

I went on board on a Monday morning and reported to the mate, a huge down-easter about forty years of age. After making a close scrutiny, he asked me if I were capable of splicing iron and other work. I replied that if he found that I was not suitable he could pay me off any time he liked, adding also that splicing iron was blacksmith's work. "I don't mean iron rods," said he, "I mean iron wire." I told him that I knew how to splice iron wire, or what we Britishers call wire rope—Gleeson could vouch for that.

At " turn-to " time the second mate, another hefty down-easter, sent us all to our various jobs. A Dutchman and I were told to take a gantline up aloft and reeve it off for a heel rope to send down the remaining part of the fore topgallant mast. Dutchy and I took up the heel rope and gantline block, hooked it on, rove the heel rope through it and through the heel of the mast, and made the end fast to the topmast cap.

When this was done the second mate called me down on deck to assist him to heave the mast high enough up to allow the fid to be drawn out. Dutchy managed to get the fid out, and called out " Lower away." I slacked away at the capstan, until the second mate called out " Avast lowering." He then roared out to Dutchy to single his heel rope and mind and rack the two parts first.

172

Dutchy put a spunyarn racking on, and when he unbent the end of the heel rope from the cap, the racking slipped and down the remaining part of the mast came by the run.   The heel struck the fore topsail yard, turned a somersault in the air, and came down on the forecastle head, the end going right through the deck, making a hole nearly three feet each way.

The mate came running out of the saloon followed by the captain.   Swearing was no name for the language which the captain and his two officers used.   Poor Dutchy nearly collapsed up aloft.   They called him down, and he almost dropped from the futtock shrouds.   I could see the lower rigging shaking as he came down gradually.   The captain ordered him ashore out of the ship right away.   Had we been at sea, or in an American port, poor Dutchy would not have got off so easily.   Dutchy lost no time in getting out of the ship as fast as his legs could carry him.

As we were discharging cargo in a rather out-of-the-way place the stevedore's men were allowed hot water from the galley to make tea.   On our second day on board, the ship's cook made a complaint owing to some of his gear having been stolen out of the galley.   The steward reported the matter to the captain, who gave instructions that the stevedore's men were, in future, not to be allowed near the galley, and no hot water was to be supplied to them.   When the men stopped work for dinner and found that there was no hot water to make tea, they went to a pompous little tally clerk and reported the matter to him.   The little man went aft to the mate right away and demanded to know why there was no hot water for the men.

" For two pins," said he to the mate, " I have a good mind to hang the ship up, and send the men ashore."

" Who are you, anyhow? " the mate asked.   " You have no authority to hang the ship up."

The little man replied : " You'll soon know who I am if I stop the ship.   One word from me, and every man will walk ashore.   Mind, you Yanks are not in America now; you are in Australia, and have Australians to deal with."

The big mate put on a sort of sheepish look which encouraged the little clerk to go over the traces; he even went so far as to walk up to the mate and shake his little fist in the mate's face, to the great amusement of the stevedore's men. The mate grabbed him immediately by the collar of the coat and seat of the trousers, and with a swing tossed him over the rail into the water. He was picked up by a steam barge which happened to be passing at the time. On seeing this, the stevedore's men all went ashore, and no more work was done that day.

The little clerk was tossed over the rails by the mate as easily as a deck swab would have been. The captain and the stevedore himself came on board in the afternoon, I suppose to patch matters up. The men returned to work next morning, and a new tally clerk came, who reported that the little man was ill in bed with a nervous breakdown.

The cook, who reported the loss of some of his gear, was an Irishman, who had been in the ship for over three years. He was known on board by the nickname of " Spike," owing to one of his forefingers being stiff in the middlejoint and resembling a marline-spike. He was a first-class cook, must have had good wages, and was very anxious to please everybody.

The Charles Dennis was, beyond doubt, a splendid living ship, and there was no comparison between her and a British ship. " Spike " reckoned that he could make a meal from a bucket of water and a bone. " Spike " gave us the full history of the ship and all on board, and what had happened on her during the three years he had been on her.

The captain was a medium-sized man about forty-five years of age, and was a typical Yank, from his goatee beard down to his square-toed boots. He had the usual sarcastic look that American captains had at that period. The cook informed us that the captain used to take doses of religion and whisky alternately. After a fairly good bout of whisky he would swear off, and take up religion to an enormous extent, but for the last twelve months or so he seemed to have dropped both recreations. About two years before our time in her, the cook informed me that she loaded a cargo of coal at Cardiff for some port in Brazil, and as she was passing out between the dock gates the officers were knocking the men about. A fairly large crowd noticed this and started booing and shouting out some " pet names " at the captain and his officers. The captain put on a bland smile, and facing the crowd he remarked, " We are all religious here in this ship and sure go to heaven."

The cook informed me that on one voyage when bound from Tal Tal to Liverpool with a cargo of nitrate of soda they had a long spell of thick foggy weather when making for the Irish Channel. The captain was not sure of the ship's position, and when off the Irish coast they came across an Irish fishing boat. The wind was very light at the time, which enabled the fishing boat to run up close alongside with the object of selling some fish. The fishermen asked the captain to buy fish or exchange fish for a bit of baccy or some salt " bafe " or pork. The captain was in a bad temper after so long a passage, and told the fishermen that he guessed and calculated that as he had been without fish for nearly 120 days he could do without fish for the rest of the voyage.

One of his officers remarked that the fishermen would have a pretty good idea where they were and suggested it advisable to ask them. He hailed the fishermen, who were then some distance off.

" Say, fishermen," said the captain, " how does the Tuskar Rock bear? "

One of the fishermen replied, " You, who are so good at guessing and calculating, can now guess and calculate the bearing and distance you are off the Tuskar."

Some time afterwards they came across some more fishermen, one of whom came close alongside and offered fish for sale. The captain struck up a bargain right away and bought enough fish to do all hands until arrival at Liverpool. He then asked whereabouts they were, and explained that he had not seen anything and was not sure of his position. The fishermen informed him that he was steering direct for the Arklow Banks, which were a few miles off. The cook said the information given by the fishermen was correct, and that was a lesson to the captain to be more civil to Irish fishermen in the future.

There was a nephew of the owner on board as a passenger, who had been sent to sea for the good of his health and to get weaned from bad company. I met him ashore in Sydney one night, and he informed me that on leaving Harvard University he had a splendid time in New York and Philadelphia, which resulted in a nervous breakdown and heart strain. He had consulted several doctors, who all advised him to stop going the pace, to get away from his companions, to take a long sea voyage, and to live a quiet life for a while. According to his account, nearly all the wealthy young men in New York went very much the same way, and were physical wrecks after leaving college.

A THOROUGHBRED OF THE SEA.

I WORKED nine days on board the Charles Dennis, and then left her to go in an Australian-owned vessel, where the pay was better. As soon as the shipping-master gave me a permit to ship, I was signed on and started work.

The vessel was over thirty years old, an Aberdeen-built wooden vessel. She had been owned by the Orient Line for a few years, and had made several record passages between England and Australia. She still kept her old speed up after going on the Australian coast. A Captain E————, who had been in command of her for several years and was in her during my time, left her about four or five years afterwards to go into steam.

We loaded a cargo of coal in Sydney for Adelaide, and had fine weather along the New South Wales coast as far as Gabo Island, when we had a succession of strong gales which made the old vessel leak like a basket. We had ten days of this weather among the islands and rocks in Bass Strait, thrashing at it all the time for all she was worth. The green seas came in over the forecastle-head in cascades, making her vibrate from stem to stern. We were standing at the pumps the greater part of the time, with ropes round us to keep us from being washed away. There we stood in water waist-deep, pumping for all we were worth. Owing to so many islands and rocks being about we often had to wear ship to clear them, and then back to the pumps again. The excessive leakage was to a certain extent caused by the hard driving which was straining the ship terribly.

On a Saturday afternoon about three o'clock we were in company with a barque called the Kingdom of Saxony, also bound to Adelaide. The wind was dead down the gulf at the time, and both ships tacked at the same time to the northward of Kingscoate (Kangaroo Island). We were up at the Semaphore Anchorage at five o'clock on Sunday morning, and the Kingdom of Saxony did not arrive there before seven o'clock on Tuesday morning.

This is a good illustration of what a smart ship commanded by a smart captain can do. Our captain probably had more local knowledge of the Gulf of St. Vincent than the other man, although the other vessel was an Adelaide trader, voyage after voyage. I have sailed in some very smart ships, but this vessel was a thoroughbred as far as sailing was concerned. I have seen her pass a large four-masted ship off Sydney Heads, when we must have done two knots for her one.

Although over thirty years of age her timbers and most of her planking were fairly sound. The vessel had been hard-driven ever since she came off the stocks at Aberdeen, and in her declining years she was driven as hard as ever during the time that Captain E——— commanded her. Captain E———, in addition to being a ship-driver, was a man-driver when it became necessary. He had rather a poor crew during the time I was with him and had to lift his hand two or three times. The vessel had the reputation of always being a leaky ship, more or less, ever since she came off the stocks. I remember when discharging coal in Adelaide the water was nearly a foot above the ceiling when she was tipped down by the head.

The coal cargo had to be discharged by the crew in Port Adelaide as this was customary in all Australian coasting vessels. One of our men, a Cockney whom we called Jack, was night-watchman during our stay in Port Adelaide. He was a steamboat man and was not much use aloft. During the rough weather in Bass Strait he was thrown over the wheel and had his wrist sprained. He was laid up during the rest of the passage, and was considered fit for nothing except night-watching.

As the captain's home was near Port Adelaide he remained away from the ship generally from four in the afternoon to nine on the following morning. One night, however, he turned up about eleven and found the watchman asleep with the ship's dog tied to his wrist. The dog apparently had gone to sleep also. The watchman was wakened with a bucket of water thrown over him. Next morning he went ashore and reported the matter to the police, who only laughed at him and refused to take any further steps in the matter.

Another Cockney by the name of Bob shammed drunk one day and wished to get paid off. He went aft and told the captain that he wished to leave as the work was too hard, and that he was both weak and lazy; and shamming drunk he fell up against the captain, who pushed him so roughly away that he fell flat on the poop. Bob called another man's attention that he had been assaulted by the captain. In order not to have any trouble in his home town the captain paid Cockney off, considering also that he was not much use in any case.

We loaded a mixed cargo in Port Adelaide for Newcastle, New South Wales, composed of tin ore, salt, chaff, and flour, and on the passage round we kept company with an Orient Liner doing about thirteen knots. If the wind had freshened up the old thoroughbred would have passed the steamer belonging to her former owners.

Like the White Star Line and the Aberdeen Line, the Orient Line started with sailing ships at first. Their first ship was the Orient, built in the early fifties, and the old ship I was in was built a year or two afterwards—a much smaller vessel but the faster, which outlived the Orient by many years. She made a record passage from Cape Horn to the Equator in twenty-one days, and was only once beaten by the Cutty Sark, and that by only a few hours. The track was laid down on the South Atlantic "blue back" charts. She also made the record that same voyage from the Equator to the Start in nineteen days, twenty-one hours. She sailed the seas for about forty years and scarcely ever had a serious accident. Her rigging was rotten when I was in her, and how it stood the strain of hard-driving was a mystery.

On the passage to Newcastle our old rigging was put to a severe test. We sighted Wilson Promontory about midnight and passed Cliffy Island about three hours later, when the wind came away strong from the north-west, which made us bowl along about thirteen knots with all sail set. About eight in the morning the weather became very thick, and the wind shifted to the south-west during a heavy rain squall. Nothing was sighted until about one in the afternoon, when Cape Everard was seen almost right ahead and about four or five miles off. It was down helm and let go weather fore braces right away, and let the fore yards run forward. Up she came to the wind, canvas flapping and chain sheets rattling.

"Take in the slack of your lee fore braces, let go weather main braces and take in the slack of the lee ones," the "Old Man" bawled out; and when the yards were braced up we were lee rails under water.

When boarding the fore tack the mate said, "She will never do it. This is the last of her after so many years. The masts will come down about our heads." He seemed to have lost his nerve, although quite a young man.

When the weather braces were well tightened up, the "Old Man" bawled out, "Set the inner and outer jibs and spanker."

When the mate heard this order given he turned pale. "Good heavens," said he, "the masts will go by the board and we will drift ashore."

When we were aft on the poop getting the spanker ready for setting, the mate remarked to the "Old Man" that too much sail was already on the ship.

"Too much sail be hanged!" said the "Old Man," "we have got to claw her off the shore somehow."

The spanker was set, and all hands told to stand-by on the poop. When we were running with the wind on the starboard quarter we scarcely felt it, but now it was quite a gale. The "Old Man" stood close by the helmsman in case he shook her up too much and something carried away.

The lee rigging and backstays were all hanging down in a bight, and the spray was going up to the foretop.

"Go it, old girl," the "Old Man" would say occasionally, "go it, you are doing it grand."

Our wake was straight behind; we were making little or no leeway. She was putting up a splendid fight; everything seemed to have a charmed life aloft until the weather main royal sheet carried away.

"Clew up the main royal and make it fast," the "Old Man" bawled out.

The main royal was clewed up, but no one would go up to make it fast except the main topgallant sail was lowered down on the lifts. The " Old Man " got into a towering rage, and ordered the mate to repair the sheet and set the sail again. The sheet was repaired and the sail was set, and Cape Everard was well astern.

After passing Gabo Island the wind was free again owing to our course being altered more to the northward. We passed every vessel going up the coast. Nothing could look at us. We arrived off Newcastle breakwater the following day about midday, and as the captain had the pilotage licence for the port we went straight into the harbour without a pilot. The vessel was shortened down to upper topsails before we came up to the breakwater.

When we were well inside the harbour, and still doing about eight knots, the harbour-master roared out, " For God's sake lower those upper topsails of yours ; you are going about eight knots in among the shipping."

" Let rip the topsail halyards, both fore and main," the " Old Man " roared out, followed by " Let go anchor."

Being an old-fashioned ship with a barrel windlass, with the chain locker alongside the main mast and only thirty fathoms of cable on deck, and doing about eight knots, something had to go. When the anchor was dropped the chain was dragged round the windlass barrel and out of the chain locker, and snapped somewhere near the thirty-fathom shackle. As soon as the cable snapped the other anchor was let go, and had it not been that a strong ebb tide was running at the time, we would have sailed right through a large Glasgow ship lying alongside the Custom House Wharf. We only cleared that vessel by a few feet. The fire was sparking from the hawse pipes before the cable snapped, and everyone expected that our bow would be ripped down to the water. Some of the men on the Glasgow ship jumped on shore, as they expected we would sail right through that vessel and bring mast and yards down about their heads.

As usual, good luck followed the old vessel in spite of mismanagement on the captain's part, who forgot to look after his ship in narrow waters in order to give the man at the wheel a mauling. We managed to claw her off Cape Everard where many ships would have landed on the beach and gone to pieces in a few minutes, with probably the loss of all hands.

Although the captain offered me the second mate's berth if I would remain in the vessel, I had decided to leave her, mostly owing to the incessant pumping in bad weather.   There is no work to do at sea so hard as jig-jogging away at the pumps for nearly two hours at a time with short intervals.   I was, however, sorry to some extent to leave the old thoroughbred of the sea, and although she was no longer an Orient Line racer she still could show a clean pair of heels and could fetch where she looked.

The last time that I saw this old vessel was in Port Pirie, South Australia, under a new captain who was still making fairly good passages.   Out of curiosity I went on board, and I was informed that she had beaten steamboat time from Brisbane to Sydney.   She had also made the passage from Port Germain to Sydney in 100 hours, which made an average of twelve knots all through.   'Tween decks had been laid since I left her which stiffened her up, and she had also been caulked fore and aft which tightened her up considerably.   Captain E——— left her to go into steam, and I was informed that he was still living in 1925, being then about 94 years of age.   His old ship was broken up in 1896, after a long and prosperous life of forty years.

CONCLUSION.

NO longer do large crowds of people assemble on the pierheads to watch the incoming ships—beautiful creations from Clyde and Aberdeen shipyards—from all parts of the world, and manned by British seamen who helped to build up the prosperity of our Empire. The sea bred a race of men who, like old Stormalong, were of the best.

The sea is still the great highway of the world, the same today as when Neco, King of Egypt, sent certain Phœnicians in ships with orders to sail down the Red Sea, down along the east coast of Africa, round the Cape of Good Hope, and back to Egypt through the Pillars of Hercules.

As time went on, ships and the men who manned them changed. The bucko Down East mate, who was a " holy terror " forty-five years ago, is no more. The belaying pin carried in the leg of the seaboot, the blackjack, the knuckle-duster, and the crimp, are all things of the past, and gone for ever. No longer the gruff old sea-dog of an English mate bawls from the poop, " Square the cro'jack yard," " lee fore brace," or " stand by royal halyards." No longer the harbours of Falmouth and Queenstown ring with the chanties of homeward-bounders.

Instead of the gruff old sea-dog of an English mate pacing fore and aft the weather side of the poop, is a spick and span uniformed officer pacing the bridge of a steamer, keeping a vigilant lookout day and night. The ultra-modern apprentice to the sea serves his time in steam and takes no interest in a sailing vessel if he should happen to see one. The sailing ship apprentice had to pay the owners a premium, which was returned to him in the shape of wages while he was serving his apprenticeship. The modern steamship apprentice pays no premium, but receives wages ranging from ten shillings to fifty shillings per month.

Quite a large number of fine sailing ships have been turned into coal hulks, stripped, with only lower masts standing. Their hulls are corroding, and black with coal dust—it is difficult even to trace their names. Their history and achievements are forgotten, and the same may be said of the men who manned them. The cities of Demerara, Rio, Santos, and Havana, have been cleaned up and turned into health resorts, and the Yellow Jack claims no more men at those ports. Refrigerators, ice-chests, cold storage, etc., have done away with " salt horse," " tinned dog," and greasy tinned beef, which put the acid test on the strongest stomach.

The clipper ship seems to be gone for ever—gone with them are our sailors.

I take my hat off to their memory.

IN "STEAM."

TO INDIA ON A NEW CLAN LINER.

IT was in the summer of 1883 that I shipped as quartermaster on a new Clan Liner bound from Glasgow to Colombo, Madras, and Calcutta. The commander was Captain John Bain, from Nairn, one of the finest men who ever commanded a ship, and a navigator second to none. He started his career in a small schooner on the Scottish coast, and through his fine personality, tact, and ability as a seaman and navigator, he was not many years at sea until he was in command in the County Line of four-masted sailing ships, and later on he was in command in the Clan Line of steamers until he retired from sea to start business as a nautical assessor.

The chief officer was also a sailing ship man and a very smart officer, who soon gained command in the Line. Later on he resigned to become a Clyde pilot and finally harbour-master at Greenock.

The Clan Macintosh was a passenger vessel, and one of the first steamers fitted with electric light. The passenger accommodation was splendid, and as good as can be found in present-day steamers. The only drawback to the first-class accommodation was that the smoke-room was away forward under the forecastle-head. The second-class accommodation was aft under the poop.

The vessel's machinery gave a lot of trouble during the whole voyage through bearings becoming heated, which necessitated the hose being played on them to cool them down. The electric light and steering gear were also breaking down occasionally. The steering chains were too light and frequently carried away, and later on a part of the steering engine broke, which rendered the steam steering gear useless, and left us nothing but the hand gear on the poop to steer with. This being the vessel's first voyage, the

M

hand gear was new and stiff—so stiff that it took two quarter-masters and four Lascars to steer the ship. The officers were put on two watches. The two juniors had to take watch and watch aft on the poop to superintend the steering. Ships carrying Lascar crews in those days carried about four times the number of men that would have been required if the whole crew had been white men.

When passing through the Suez Canal all vessels had to make fast as sunset and start away again at sunrise. The canal pilots were mostly Frenchmen, Italians, and Greeks, and a more excitable lot it would be hard to find anywhere. I was at the wheel leaving Port Said (our steam stearing gear had not broken down at this time), and as soon as we entered the canal the French pilot started with his eternal " port," " port leetle more," " ay stedy," " ay starbor," " ay hardy, starbor," " amidships." Consequently the canal was too narrow for us. He commenced tearing his hair and stamping from one end of the bridge to the other, and cried out, " Relievy day wheel mistro mate, dees boy no ay steer, day ship go ashore."

As my mate was laid up with sore eyes and the other two quartermasters were off watch, the third officer had to run down and report to the captain that the pilot wanted the wheel relieved immediately. The captain came up on the bridge and took the wheel for about five minutes. " Now," said he to me, " steer the ship straight ; keep a buoy on each bow and don't give her too much helm."

I took the wheel again and kept the vessel going straight, and after a while the pilot came along and remarked, " What for you no ay steeri day ship like dat at feerst ? " I told him that it was owing to being messed about by him. That pilot gave me no more trouble.

At Ismailia we changed pilots, and the new pilot, who was either a Greek or an Italian, started on to one of the other quartermasters who was at the wheel when he came on board. The man at the wheel lost his temper, and the consequence was the ship bumped against the bank very heavily. When the pilot saw we were to strike the canal bank he ordered the wheel hard a-starboard, and when she hit the bank only slightly she sheered across to the other side of the canal with the helm still hard a-starboard and struck very heavily. The captain came running up on the bridge, and as the pilot had lost his head completely the captain manoeuvred the ship into the fairway again.

Coming down the Red Sea the heat was terrific. The Lascar firemen and coal trimmers were completely exhausted in the stoke-hold, and several had to be hauled up from below in a helpless condition. Deck hands had to assist below in order to keep the steam up. The temperature in the engine-room was considerably over 120 degrees. Several of the passengers were prostrated by the heat and many were on the point of collapsing. The heat remained very oppressive until we reached the Gulf of Aden, when it gradually cooled down, and on reaching Cape Guardafui it was fairly cool on deck. When under the lee of Cape Guardafui millions of locusts blew on board; every shroud and rope, even the signal halyards, were covered with them, from the trucks at the mastheads down to the decks. Every cabin in the ship had large numbers of locusts, under the berths, on the beds, among clothes, in drawers if any happened to be open, inside boots and shoes, and in wash-basins if any water happened to be in them.

Once we passed Cape Guardafui we had the full force of the south-west monsoon, with a heavy beam sea, which we experienced all the way to Colombo. Owing to the strong monsoon all port-holes had to be kept closed to keep the water out of the cabins, which made a stifling heat all over the passenger accommodation. Owing to the strong wind all the awnings had to be kept furled, which exposed the passengers to heavy sprays of salt water and a broiling sun overhead. There was very little comfort in travelling by sea in those days; there were no electric fans to cool the berths and saloons, and no ice-water.

The breakwater at Colombo was not completed at this time, consequently the harbour was very exposed to wind and sea at times. When lying in Colombo Harbour, divers used to go down to gather up pieces of coal which had fallen into the water from ships discharging coal. They stood on a large egg-shaped stone weighing nearly one hundred pounds. A hole was bored through the stone large enough to take a piece of two-and-a-quarter-inch rope. Before descending, the diver put a small pair of wooden clams over his nostrils to keep the water out, and then stood on the stone and was lowered to the bottom by his mates in the boat. He generally remained down from three to four minutes at a time, when he gave the signal to his mates to haul up. When he came to the surface he had to spit out blood occasionally. The basket containing the coal was hauled up by a separate rope which the man took down with him. I presume those divers were allowed to keep the coal obtained in this manner. Although there are plenty of sharks in those waters, they do not seem to have troubled the divers.

Our next port of call was Madras, where we had to lie in an exposed roadstead, rolling so heavily that passengers coming on board had to get into a large coal basket which was hove up by the steam winch and landed on deck.

The passage from Madras to the Sand Heads was fairly fine, and we arrived at the pilot brig about nine o'clock on a Sunday forenoon. The Calcutta pilots at that time were great Burra Sahibs; no Spanish Grandee, Indian Potentate, or Chinese Mandarin, could be compared with them and the dignified airs they put on. One would imagine when one of those pilots came on board that he was the Lord of Creation. Since 1883 I have visited mostly every country in the world, and during all my travels I never came across a man I could compare to one of those white nabobs. He came alongside with a boatload of baggage, which took the crew some time to haul up the ship's side. With his pure white gloves, solo topee, and immaculate white suit, he was very pleased with himself. He was accompanied by his leadsman and his servant whom he called "boy"—generally an old man with a long grey beard, who had to stand at attention nearly all the time. He (the pilot) expected everybody on board to kow-tow to him—even the captain of the vessel. He was not long on board before he called out, "Boy, boy, brandy and sowda low." His leadsman was an apprentice pilot who had put in a couple of years as a cadet in the Conway or Worcester, and if he had not a long pedigree he was despised by the others. The Calcutta pilots in the early eighties were not above taking a gratuity, although it was against the rules. They were stationed on board smart little brigs, off the Sand Heads, which could be manoeuvred very easily. They could back and fill and turn round almost within their own length.

As I have already mentioned, our steam steering gear was out of commission, and we had to fall back on our hand gear aft on the poop, which was still very stiff and almost unworkable. It took two quartermasters and about seven or eight Lascars all their time to turn it quickly enough in the river. When nearing the James and Mary the vessel took a sheer, and before we could meet her with the hand gear she was ashore.

A tug going past was offered one thousand rupees to pull us off. He, however, took no notice but went on his way. We remained hard and fast all night and came off ourselves next forenoon about nine o'clock. A few minutes afterwards we grounded on a bank and after going nearly over on our beam ends, slipped off again. As soon as the vessel slipped off the bank she became upright again and we proceeded up the river to Calcutta without any further mishap. Calcutta was still a very sickly port at that time, with cholera, smallpox, malaria, jungle fever, diarrhoea, and dysentery. I had the misfortune to go down with cholera, which came on very suddenly. The pain is terrific, and after a short time the patient becomes delirious and cannot straighten himself out, but must lie with his knees drawn up towards his chin. My case most probably would have been serious if it had not been taken in time. Being a passenger ship we carried a doctor, who was on the spot as soon as I became ill. Calcutta River (Hooghly) was responsible for a large amount of illness on board ships at this particular time. The health authorities recommended that ships' awnings should be laced to the rails during the night, so that the crews would not be exposed to the night haze and dampness off the river.

It was nothing unusual to see a dozen bodies of human beings floating past during the day, and a vulture feasting on each. Those vultures are very large birds of a dark brown colour, are the scavengers of the river—like the street dogs in Constantinople— and have a voracious manner of eating. The bodies often got doubled up across ships' cables and hung there for some time, until the crew pushed them clear, when they again continued their journey down the river with the tide.   It was therefore no wonder that cholera was so prevalent in Calcutta.

Boys going to Calcutta for the first time often fall victims to cholera through drinking cheap lemonade with a piece of ice in it. The boys get thirsty through walking about the streets on a hot evening and get drinking this trashy stuff from a native lemonade shop.   The boys like it, it is fine and sweet, and the lump of ice makes it cool and refreshing.   It was the Calcutta lemonade which gave me cholera.   Any stranger going to an Indian port should avoid drinking any kind of native drinks—even clean water is dangerous if taken to excess.   Fruit in those days was always a carrier of cholera and smallpox through being handled by so many people before reaching the consumer.

A good cure for cholera in those days was : To three-quarters of a bottle of brandy add two dessertspoonsful of laudanum and four dessertspoonsful of white pepper, all to be well shaken, and the patient to get a tablespoonful every two hours.   I have used this and found it very successful.   Malaria was spread among ships' crews through the agency of mosquitoes, sixty per cent. of them being reckoned as malaria carriers.

At the change of the monsoons the weather is very unsettled. The rain comes down in torrents, and shortly afterwards a broiling sun comes out.   Smallpox is not so prevalent during the rainy season owing to the sewers being well flushed out with rain water. It is during the dry season in most tropical countries that smallpox is most prevalent.

The white men treated the natives very badly at this time. Ships' officers and seamen used to treat the coolies working on board most brutally.   The coolie had to work ten hours a day on board a ship for the magnificent sum of half a rupee (one shilling) per day.   They were chased around, kicked, and sworn at by ships' officers and foremen stevedores.   We had a considerable amount of heavy iron pipes and girders on board which required skilful handling, under the supervision of a West Indian negro, who mauled the poor coolies most unmercifully. Sailormen on shore also treated the natives very badly.

We carried four white men as greasers in the engine-room, who were always committing some depredations on shore and getting locked up. There was a drinking saloon not far from where the ship lay, kept by a native called Bombay Jack, where the British tar could be seen any hour of the day. One day two of our greasers went in there and helped themselves to a bottle of whisky apiece. Bombay Jack remonstrated with them, and was promptly struck over the head with one of the bottles which laid him unconscious on the floor outside his counter. The two rascals then took to their heels and made for the ship as quickly as their legs could carry them, and managed to get on board.

About an hour afterwards a white police officer, accompanied by four native policemen, came down to arrest them. Although both men were nearly drunk by this time, they put up a hard fight; the white policeman was struck on the head with a spanner. The cut was a severe one, the back of his white suit was almost covered with blood and his head had to be stitched by the ship's doctor. Both men were handcuffed, and had to be carried ashore and put into a cab. They were sentenced to three months' imprisonment. It turned out afterwards that they had robbed and cheated almost everyone they had come in contact with.

The bumboat man was Sam Doss, who supplied us with eggs, fruit, cigars, matches, etc. As old Sam Doss could neither read nor write English he had to trust to every man's honour. The two greasers, first of all, did not put their proper names down, and afterwards did not state the correct amount of goods received. Old Sam became suspicious and came to us (quartermasters) to read over the entries the greasers had made in the book. We read everything over to him, and remarked that the men had not given their correct names so far as we knew. Old Sam went over to them and asked them why they had tried to cheat him. With tears in his eyes, he said, " Me poor man, sahib, you rich man get plenty good money, what for you try cheat me? " One of the men asked for the book so that he could make it right. When Old Sam handed him the book he tore it in two and pitched it into the river.

The two greasers received a thrashing from one of the quarter-masters, and we told Sam to bring another book down and we would make new entries as truthfully as we possibly could.

It was a common practice in those days for sailormen to take long drives through the town in gharrys, and when nearing the ship they would jump off unobserved, one at a time, and when the gharry wallah reached his destination he would find an empty gharry and no pay. There was a steamer lying close to us with a tough Liverpool crew who made themselves the terror of the riverside. Three or four of those rascals had a long drive through Calcutta one Sunday, and when near the General Post Office on their return journey the gharry wallah stopped and remarked that as they had only a short distance to go they could easily walk that far. The men refused to pay and threatened the man instead. The gharry wallah agreed to drive them to the ship's side, but instead of taking them there he drove away at a gallop to a back street, stopped his gharry, and before the men knew where they were they were hauled out on to the street and surrounded by a crowd of angry coolies armed with bamboos. The men were so severely beaten that two of them had to be taken to hospital; if the police had not arrived on the scene in time, most probably they would have been beaten to death.

We spent nearly three weeks in Calcutta, and called again at Madras and Colombo on our way home, and arrived in London about Christmas time.

ACROSS THE ATLANTIC.

IN January, 1884, I shipped as an A.B. in a passenger liner bound from Glasgow to New York. We were ordered on board at 0.5 a.m., *viz.*, five minutes past midnight. This is a most unusual time to order men to join a ship; however, we had to comply with the time read out to us from the ship's articles.

At eleven o'clock three of us drove away from the Sailors' Home in the cart belonging to that institution with our baggage and bedding, and when we arrived alongside the vessel the watchman at the gangway would not allow us on board. We explained that we were ordered on board at five minutes past midnight. "Captain orders," said the watchman, "no one allowed on board until six in the morning." We had to drive back to the Sailors' Home, baggage and all.

Arrangements were made to start away from the Home at half past five, but owing to one of the other men not being up in time it was five minutes past six before we left, and it was about half past six before we had our baggage on board. Through not being on board at six we were logged a day's pay, although we started work at seven o'clock that morning and worked all day up to midnight.

We left Glasgow at eleven o'clock that night, and we anchored at the Tail of the Bank sometime about three o'clock next morning. The Superintendent of the Line was on the bridge going down the river, and was not backward in letting himself be heard.

The night was fine but pitch-dark, and drunken men were falling over hatches and other gear scattered all over the ship's decks. We were employed all night in cleaning up and coiling away hauling lines, mooring wire, sweeping and washing decks. One drunken fireman fell down a forecastle stair and broke one of his legs, which accident was followed by several fights amongst the other firemen. The chief officer gave the bos'n instructions to ship the brass nozzle on to the wash-deck hose and scatter them.

193

This had the desired effect. None of them could face the piercing stream of water which was played on their faces.

About eleven o'clock in the forenoon all the seamen had to muster to boat drill. Two boats were swung out and lowered into the water and rowed round the ship. The third officer took charge of the port boat and the fourth officer was in charge of the starboard boat. Before going into the boats, the boats' crews had to put their lifebelts on (instead of getting into the boats first and then putting them on). Several men had never seen lifebelts before and did not know the proper way to put them on, and how to fix them when they were on. When our boat was being lowered into the water the after-gear took a run, and the consequence was the boat was hanging by the bow-gear only—almost perpendicularly. The gear was faulty, and had the vessel been at sea with the boat full of passengers the greater part of them would have fallen into the water.

When we started to row around the ship, it appeared that two of our men had never had an oar in their hands before. One of them caught a " crab " and lost his oar; the other man's oar was always fouling the oar of the man pulling behind him. We rowed round the ship somehow and came back to our boat's davits.

Weighing anchor, we proceeded to sea that evening and arrived at Moville on the following afternoon.

While on the passage round to Moville all of us who failed to join the ship in Glasgow at six o'clock in the morning were brought along to the purser's room and fined one day's pay.

Several of us protested against the injustice, and pointed out to the chief officer that we had worked all day in Glasgow from seven o'clock in the morning right up to midnight, and from one o'clock on the following morning until five in the evening without a break.

The chief officer was inexorable, and remarked that it did not matter how long we had worked afterwards. " The point is," said he, " you did not turn to at six in the morning." One man remarked, " You will be sorry for this yet, mister." The chief officer instructed the purser to log the man again five shillings for giving insolence to his superior officer. " Five shillings every time you open your mouth and speak in a disrespectful manner to an officer. Have you anything else to say?" the chief officer inquired. The man replied he had nothing else to say.

A motley crowd of passengers came on board at Moville with their straw beds and tin utensils. Some of them had a sackful of straw instead of a bed to sleep on. Some were nearly drunk, and sang " Come back to Erin " and " Kathleen Mavourneen." Being winter-time we did not have more than about 250 passengers. After leaving Moville a stowaway turned up. Although a diligent search had been made by the fourth officer and a quartermaster for the deck department, and by the engineers in the parts of the ship under their jurisdiction, the man managed to conceal his where-abouts. He was brought before the captain and stated that he secreted himself on board in Glasgow about the fiddley.

The chief engineer was sent for immediately, and the captain asked him why his staff had been so careless in making their search for stowaways, as the stowaway stated that he was stowed away somewhere about the fiddley. " Come along," said the chief engineer, " and show me where you hid yourself." The stowaway pointed out the place to the captain, chief engineer, and chief officer where he said he had been, and had remained all the time since he came on board. " You are a liar," said the chief engineer. " You go in there again and let us see how you can stand it." The stowaway walked in and the chief engineer closed the iron door on him. He had not been in more than five minutes before he commenced hammering on the iron door and begged to be let out.

The place was a small compartment around the funnel which the sailors and firemen called a drying-room, where they used to dry their clothes. When the man was let out of this room he almost collapsed on the deck. " That shows that the man is a liar," said the chief engineer to the captain. " He could not have lived in that place all the time since leaving Glasgow."

The man declared to us that he had been there all the time, only he kept the door partly open as a rule. He stated that he was American born, and such being the case he could not be imprisoned on arrival in New York. A man cannot be imprisoned in the United States for trying to ride on the cheap, either on a

train or on a ship.   In the case of a vessel entering a United States
port with a stowaway on board belonging to any country outside
the United States he can be put in prison until that vessel sails
again, when he must be taken away anywhere out of the country.
The law in Great Britain is different.   All stowaways are liable to
be sentenced to from a month to two months' imprisonment, and if
they are foreigners they must be deported.

There were about eighteen to twenty nondescript able seamen
in this vessel belonging to various countries, and about six of them
did not seem to be sailors at all.   In addition to these there were
six quartermasters, bos'n, bos'n's mate, storekeeper, maindeck man,
and lamp-trimmer.

The chief officer belonged to the Shetland Islands, and had
formerly commanded a fine sailing ship.   He was a man about
forty years of age, and a man-driver.   The second officer was a
Caithness man, and also a hard case, and used to spar before the
mirror in his room.   The third and fourth officers were both
elderly men.   All officers in those ships had to be men of experience ; young men without experience could not obtain employment
in that Line.   The captain was a fairly old man, who left everything
in connection with the working of the ship in the hands of the chief
officer.

Being winter-time we had the usual North Atlantic weather all
the way across to New York.   We commenced the voyage with
head winds, sometimes blowing hard, then it would ease down for
a few hours, and then freshen up often harder than ever.   As soon
as the wind would haul a little out on either bow trysails were set,
and perhaps in less than an hour's time had to be taken in again.
The vessel was square-rigged on the fore and main, and as soon as
those squaresails would draw they were set.

One evening about seven o'clock these squaresails were set
owing to the wind being on the port beam.   About two hours
afterwards the wind shifted right ahead in a snow squall, and the
sails had to be clewed up again.   It took all hands nearly three
hours up aloft on the yards to furl those sails.   When I mention
all hands I mean all the men who could be found, as five or six
men were hidden away somewhere.   There were also two men

on the lookout who had to remain there. I had the misfortune to be up on the main mast, and owing to the wind being rather ahead we were nearly smothered with the smoke from the funnels, in addition to the snow. The sails were all aback against the masts and it was impossible to get hold of a slack part of canvas. Two men got their fingers frostbitten up aloft that night.

The wind remained at the north-west for the rest of the passage and the cold was very intense. The saltwater spray became frozen on the ship's rigging and decks. Sometimes there was ice two feet in depth on the forecastle-head, and the ropes coated so thickly with it that they would be four times their original thickness. There was no holystoning or washing down decks during the latter part of the passage. The weather became colder as we neared New York, and when we arrived there it was twenty-one degrees below zero.

The steerage passengers were examined on board by the port doctors. Each passenger had to show his vaccination marks, the doctor then turned down his eyelids, and the medical examination was complete. Any passenger who had not sufficient clothing or was without a certain amount of money was not allowed to remain in the United States. Two of our passengers were found to be short of the necessary amount of money and clothing to meet the requirements of the United States immigration authorities, and were considered paupers. The Line were held responsible and had to repatriate those passengers. We had great difficulty in getting alongside the pier owing to the large amount of field-ice coming down the River Hudson.

As soon as we were moored alongside, most of the firemen and coal-trimmers made for the shore and up to a drinking saloon called the " Clipper." They were on the spree during the whole time the ship lay in New York, and each man had to pay three dollars per day for a substitute. They generally came on board about midnight, and when they reached their forecastle a fight was sure to take place shortly afterwards. One night three of them went along to the galley and demanded tea or coffee from the quarter-master, and when the quartermaster refused, one of them picked

up a kettle of boiling coffee and threw it over him and burned him
very severely, so much so that he had to be sent to hospital.

Ships' firemen—especially those in the North Atlantic liners—
were the most incorrigible lot of men going to sea. They were a
law unto themselves, and when they arrived in port they went
ashore and got drunk, and did no work so long as they could raise
the price of a drink. They never had much clothes, but what
little they had was sold for drink. Most of our firemen seemed
to be married men, whose wives had to stand outside the shipping
office in Glasgow so as to meet them as soon as they came out with
their pay in their pockets.

At this particular time there used to be a public-house at the
corner of James Watt Street and the Broomielaw, where the
firemen took in their wives and children to have a drink after
leaving the pay-table. This public-house must have been a gold
mine to its owner. I understand that one of the leading shipowners of Glasgow bought the whole corner out and converted
the public-house into a shop of some kind.

Seamen and firemen did not fraternize in those days. There
was nothing in common between them, even if they had sailed
together for several voyages. It did not matter how rough a
sailorman was, he considered himself far above a fireman.

There used to be a notorious boarding-house keeper in New
York during the early eighties called " Hell Fire Jack," who kept a
house somewhere about Mulberry Street or Cherry Street, on the
east side of the city, and whose name was familiar on the seven
seas.

This gentleman paid us a visit on the evening of our arrival in
New York. He introduced himself as " Hell Fire Jack," and said
he was proud of the name people called him. He was a powerfully
built man, slightly over six feet, and very expensively dressed.
His overcoat had a fur collar about six inches deep, and he had
three or four diamond rings on his fingers which must have cost
several hundred dollars. He said that he wanted several men for
an American ship bound from New York to Rio de Janeiro. No
one cared about going to Rio owing to its being a white man's
grave in those days. He said that he also wanted a full crew of

fourteen men for an English vessel bound to Australia, as well as some men for an American steamer in the Panama trade. He managed to coax eight or nine men away, whom he promised to get berths for in steamers trading to the Gulf of Mexico. The men left that night and none of us knew what became of them.

During all the time that we lay in New York the cold was terrific. The wads of cotton waste almost froze in our hands when we were washing the white paintwork. The cold weather was not taken into consideration so far as our work was concerned.

There were no electric tramway cars in New York in those days. All the street cars were drawn by horses, and straw was spread over the floors of the cars to keep people's feet warm. Notices were stuck up in all cars to beware of pickpockets.

AMONG THE "PACKET RATS."

ALL passenger liners sailed from New York on Saturdays, generally about from eleven o'clock in the forenoon up to one o'clock in the afternoon. About eight new men joined on Saturday morning to take the places of those who deserted, and a hard-looking crowd they were. Six of them would have been over forty-five years of age, and said that they had spent their young days in the packet ships in the Liverpool and New York trade. The men who manned those ships were known as "Packet Rats"; their headquarters were in Bootle and Scotland Road, in Liverpool. The men came on board as they stood up, and, as usual, they went ashore at the end of the voyage with a fairly good rigout.

In addition to the six "Packet Rats" there was another old "Packet Rat" about sixty years of age, who was known as Garry Owen, "the terror of the Western Ocean." He claimed to have the honour of being Garry Owen himself, which statement was corroborated by his mates. He stated that he had been in the packet ships nearly all his life, until they ceased to run owing to the steamers cutting them out of the trade. When he left sail he went into the National Line of steamers. His mates stated that he never wore boots, no matter how cold the weather was, and that he always managed to get clothes from his shipmates, who took pity on him. He said himself that every penny he earned was spent in drink. As it was winter-time we all gave him a rigout on the day after leaving New York.

He informed me that he made a voyage from New York to San Francisco, sometime in the fifties, when the Californian gold rush was on, with the notorious Bully Sanders in a fine new ship, either on her first or second voyage. There was no railway across the American Continent in those days, and the only way to reach the gold fields of California was around Cape Horn in sailing ships. This vessel, commanded by Bully Sanders, had a large number of passengers on board, and carried about sixty seamen.

Old Garry Owen described Bully Sanders as a tiger with a human body, who had murdered dozens of men. His officers were almost as brutal as himself. Bully Sanders, old Garry stated, was not a powerfully built man, but he was still young and very active, and was therefore a tough customer when he had a black-jack in his hand. He and his officers never used bare fists to a man; the black-jack or the belaying pin carried in the leg of the seaboot were always in evidence.

A Captain E———, a stevedore in New York, knew Sanders very well, and informed me that he was the greatest fraud of a man he ever knew. With a very refined, pale face, and low, soft-spoken voice, he reckoned this tiger could deceive an archangel. The stevedore told me that a cousin of his was chief mate with Sanders on a voyage from New York to 'Frisco, and when only a few days out from New York the relations between them became very strained, which ended in a fight one day in the saloon, and Bully Sanders was not seen on deck for nearly a week.

The mate had a fairly good idea that Sanders was scheming how he could manage to get even with him, and was always on his guard at all times. Sanders became extremely sociable, and one day he remarked to the mate that this little bit of trouble between them was getting on his nerves, and his earnest wish was to let bygones be bygones. Let us drink one another's health. Two glasses of grog were poured out, and Sanders instead of drinking stood with the glass in his hand, talking, so as to give the mate time to drink his. The mate, however, was not to be caught, but stood, glass in hand, listening, and remarked later on that the captain had better drink first. Both left the grog untouched—it was a drawn game. After arrival in San Francisco the mate was sandbagged one night by some boarding-house runners, and packed off that same night on an American ship bound for Havre. Bully Sanders got even with his mate after all.

The other six rascals (" Packet Rats ") began helping themselves to other people's clothes. One night, just after leaving New York, I went into the forecastle to get my overcoat as I had to go and keep a lookout on the forward lookout bridge. As after searching all over the forecastle I could not find it, I had to go

N

on the lookout without it.   Next day I noticed one of the men
on the lookout bridge with my overcoat on.   As soon as he came
down I ordered him to take that coat off.   The truculent rascal
brazened it out and declared the coat was his.   I could see that
physical force was required if I were to obtain possession of the
coat, and when he saw that he was going to get thrashed he took
the coat off and handed it back to me.

One night a young Swede turned out of his bunk at one bell
and found a good pair of leather seaboots missing.   Next day he
noticed that one of the " Packet Rats " was working on deck with
them on.   He went and demanded his seaboots at once.   " Get out,
you square-head," the " Packet Rat " exclaimed, " those boots are
mine."   " What is the matter? " asked one of his mates.
" Matter! " said the other.   " This joker of a square-head says
that these seaboots are his."   " Well," said his mate, " he has got
a hide, seeing that I was with you when you bought them at
Lewis's, and paid thirty-five bob for them.   If you don't go for
him, I will."   The consequence was the poor Swede was done out
of his boots, and most of his best clothes besides.

Several other members of the crew lost clothes and never saw
them again, the " Packet Rats " having hid them away somewhere.
I never saw men who could brazen it out like those men, but when
it came to fighting they could not stand up to those young men
whom they had been robbing.   They often talked about using the
knife when their honesty was doubted, and this seemed to scare
some of the younger men, especially the Scandinavians.   All their
talk was about killing hard-case mates in the packet ships, so as to
frighten us younger men.

Three days after leaving New York I was promoted to quartermaster, in place of the quartermaster who was scalded when the
fireman threw the kettle of boiling coffee over him.   After this I
saw very little of the " Packet Rats " except when heaving the log.

Owing to the weather being very cold, poor old Garry Owen
was laid up nearly all the way across.   The old man was done, and
unfit to go to sea any longer.   Owing to his having sailed so long
in the packet ships (which were under the American flag) he was
an eligible candidate to enter the Sailors' Snug Harbour on Staten

Island. This is a most magnificent building where seamen of all nations can find refuge provided they can prove that they have sailed four years on American-owned ships flying the American flag.

I visited the place in 1900, and I was informed that there were 800 seamen living there at that time. All that part of New York around Madison Square, I was informed, was left by some wealthy gentleman for the upkeep and support of the Snug Harbour which he had built. The inmates are well fed and clad, and the surroundings are beautiful. The grounds are laid out in terraces, and beautiful flowers grow all over the place. Garry Owen was in this place, but owing to his incorrigible disposition and drunken habits he was turned out of it and had to go to sea again.

The other " Packet Rats " were malingerers, and owing to the ship's surgeon being a young man newly from the university, he was bluffed very easily when he had experienced old rascals like those to deal with.

The weather was rough all the way across, but every opportunity was taken to holystone decks if it was at all possible. The holystoning of decks was always done during the night in those ships, when no passengers were about. At nine o'clock the men went to coffee. At nine-thirty they started holystoning decks until midnight, when they went below. The other watch holystoned decks until three o'clock in the morning, when they started washing decks down.

The holystones are fixed in iron frames with a handle about five feet long, and are pushed backwards and forwards over the deck which has been sanded beforehand. One bright moonlight night we were running before a heavy sea and shipping large quantities of water at times, and about ten o'clock a big sea came over where the men were holystoning. Every man dropped his stone when he saw the big grey-beard was to tumble on the top of him and made a race for the alleyway. As soon as the deck was again clear of water some of them rushed along and threw holystones, buckets and brooms all over the side. The bos'n, who was forward at the time the big sea came over, came aft and found all the men standing in the alleyway. " What is the matter? " said he. " Holystones all washed over the side," said one man. Another said that he was nearly washed overboard, and was half way out between the rails.

The bos'n having given orders to get more stones up from below, holystoning went on again the same as usual. He (the bos'n), however, was careful to remain where the work was going on until midnight. When the old bos'n's mate and his watch came on deck, holystones, buckets and brooms could not be found anywhere. " Someone must have thrown them overboard again," the bos'n's mate remarked to the bos'n, who was a very excitable man from Cork. " Be jabbers," said the bos'n, " I would give my pay-day to know who threw those stones overboard."

One of the " Packet Rats " remarked to the bos'n that he knew who threw the stones overboard. " Who was it ? " the bos'n asked. The " Packet Rat " replied that the Liverpool fellow did it, the same fellow who took the stones out of the frames and holystoned decks for a whole watch with an empty cigar box instead of a stone. " Which Liverpool fellow did that ? " the bos'n asked. The " Packet Rat " replied, " The one who steers the ship when lying in port, and grinds water for the captain's ducks."

This did not put an end to the holystoning of decks, as there were still a few found in the sand-locker.

A considerable amount of painting was done at night-time in the alleyways, and firemen coming up from the stokehold used to disfigure the wet paint with their black hands. One night the chief officer caught a fireman placing both his black hands on the new paint, and called his mate's attention to it. " Look at that," he said to his mate. " And look at this," the chief officer remarked when he gave the fireman a swinging blow which laid him out on the deck.

On the passage home the cooks were very busy during the night boiling down salt beef and pork for the fat the meat contained. The meat was thrown overboard afterwards. The same lot of cooks would not give a passenger a pannikin of hot water unless he was paid for it. To stop this rascally business of boiling down meat for its fat, the Line gave the cooks what was called " fat money " instead.

On the passage home one of the first-class passengers became insane through excessive drinking. His brother, who was with him, stated that the insane man was an American judge. One seaman had to remain beside him all the time in case he tried to commit suicide, either by jumping overboard or by cutting his throat. The man, however, was quite harmless. At eight bells the bos'n or bos'n's mate always piped the watch on deck and called out, " Relieve the watch, a hand on the lookout, a hand to the fresh water pump, and a hand to the madman."

On the passage out to New York a first-class passenger was caught in the act of trying to cut his throat with a blunt table-knife, which he took out of the pantry. The pantryman happened to see him in time and managed to get the knife out of his hand. The wound was stitched up by the ship's surgeon right away, and the man was able to walk ashore in New York.

One rough night a young Irishman told the passengers in the second class that the ship was expected to founder at eleven p.m. promptly, which caused a panic among them. Several rushed for the stairway, and had it not been for the steward, who was standing in the second-class pantry at the time, something serious would have happened. Some of the grown-up men ran up the stairway and were nearly washed over the side, and several women in their nightdresses rushed out of their rooms and fainted, and children screamed.

The weather had been very rough all day, and passengers were not allowed on deck in case they were injured by the sea or washed overboard. The chief steward went up to the bridge and reported the matter to the senior officer of the watch, who gave orders to the junior officer of the watch to take a quartermaster with him and bring the young Irishman up on the bridge. I was the quartermaster who went down into the second-class accommodation along with the junior officer, and when we reached the foot of the stairway there were still a lot of wild-eyed, panic-stricken men, women and children standing there.

The officer was an elderly and experienced-looking man whose commanding appearance acted like oil on troubled waters. " My good people," he said, " calm yourselves, this ship could weather any gale or sea that ever ran; there is no danger whatever, I assure you.   Go to your rooms and make yourselves comfortable."

The officer then demanded that the young man who hoaxed the passengers should be brought along to him.   He, however, had hidden himself in an empty room, and it took the second-class steward and pantryman some time before they found him.   The officer and I brought him up to the bridge before the commander. The man stated that he hoaxed the people for sport, and that he never expected that anyone would believe the hoax.   The commander gave orders that he should be handcuffed and stand on the bridge for two hours.

When we arrived at the Tail of the Bank two detectives came on board and arrested two first-class passengers, who, by all accounts, were the most expert burglars and safe-breakers in the United States.

One of them was a short, stout man, about forty years of age or thereabouts, and had such a fatherly appearance that he was a great favourite with the half dozen or so of children in the first-class saloon.   The other man was much younger, tall, thin, with black beard and piercing black eyes.   He asked me one night if it was certain that the ship would anchor at the Tail of the Bank, or would she go straight up to Glasgow.   Being my first voyage in the trade I could not give him the information he required.   By the man's look I considered that he was quite capable of committing any crime.

We arrived at Glasgow in due course.   It was customary in those days to pay off crews at the Mercantile Marine Office, and not on board as at present.   All hands were requested to be at the shipping office at two p.m.

About an hour before the appointed time, I should say there were about ten or twelve women waiting, some with young children carried in arms, and children from two to five years old hanging on to their skirts.   Most of the women had a starved, pale and haggard appearance.   They were very poorly dressed, and all had shawls over their heads.   They had come to get a few shillings from their husbands as soon as they came out with their money.   If they did not catch them then, their chances of getting any money afterwards would be very small. All those women had come to meet the stokehold hands. Most of the seamen did not live in Glasgow, and probably were not married men at all. Most sailormen of those days were bachelors.

At two o'clock the ship's purser and officers came along and handed each man his account of wages to check before he went in to the pay-table. One sailorman was too drunk to understand how much money was due him, and called out to his mate (who was about as drunk as himself) to come and see if his account of wages was all right. Three or four men were so intoxicated that the shipping office official refused to give them their money. On hearing this, the men became so abusive that the policeman belonging to the building had to put them on to the street. Nearly all the firemen were drunk and off duty in New York, which meant that two pounds ten shillings had to be deducted off their pay.

At this particular time stern discipline was maintained on board all passenger ships, whether steam or sail. It was no place for a man who could not keep sober or would not submit to discipline. The handspike and belaying pin were never used on board these vessels. The official log-book took their places. If a man was insolent to an officer, or went ashore without leave, or was drunk and disorderly, or disobeyed any lawful command, his pocket was the loser.

The officers on those ships were very arbitrary and overbearing in their manner towards the men. What I saw of the men on the ship I was in (with the exception of the " Packet Rats ") they were physically and morally good men, so far as I could judge by their conversation and manners.

The firemen could not be considered as seamen in those days; most of them probably were grown-up men before they went to sea, and consequently could never understand the cast-iron discipline maintained by the executive officers.

The same discipline is maintained on passenger liners of the present day.

In American passenger ships, and cargo ships, there was very poor discipline ten years ago; every man was a law unto himself, worked only when he felt like it, went ashore and stayed away from the ship as long as he liked.   American ships have changed since Bully Sanders' time.

Quartermasters had a fairly good time in the North Atlantic liners of those days.   The steering of the ship was the most important duty they had to perform, and the man who could not keep the ship within five degrees on each side of her course was considered unfit for the job.   Their other duties were to keep the chart-room and wheelhouse clean, clean all brasswork on the bridge, look after all the flags and keep them in proper repair.   Log lines, lead lines, patent logs, etc., are all under the quartermasters' care also.   In some Lines the quartermasters have to bring the officers' coffee on the bridge to them every two hours during the night, and in other Lines one of the night stewards does this.   In port the quartermasters do gangway duty, day and night.   They must be expert helmsmen and leadsmen—in short, they must be first-class men in every respect—sober, honest, and reliable, as they hold a position of trust.   During the time of which I write, those men were most frightfully underpaid; their wages were only ten shillings per month more than the able seaman.

I threw up my job as quartermaster on arrival at Glasgow, for several reasons—the principal being that I wished to go back in sail and not waste any time in steam.   I wanted to get my sea-time in as soon as possible so that I could go up for a second mate's certificate.   I had a fairly good ground-work in navigation and nautical astronomy before I went to sea, which helped me to pass four examinations, *viz.*, from second mate to extra master, very easily.

In those days all officers on liners held square-rig certificates. They usually remained in sail until they obtained their masters' certificates, and then started at the bottom rung of the ladder as junior officers on liners.   Most of the leading companies then preferred their junior officers, when joining, to have reached the age of thirty or thereabouts.

The officers on North Atlantic liners had a very hard time in the early eighties.   They were underpaid, had long hours on duty, and promotion was very slow.   Third and fourth officers had to berth together in a miserably small cabin, so small that one had to

lie in his bed until the other washed and dressed and went out
of the room.   There was practically no ventilation to those small
cabins except what came in through the doors, which could only be
kept on the hooks during fine weather and when no passengers were
about.

In Glasgow, on sailing day, the junior officers had to be on board
for duty at six in the morning, and would be on their feet for the
next forty hours or so.   Some years afterwards I was a junior
officer in a North Atlantic liner, and sometimes had to do fifty
hours' duty without a break, for the magnificent wage of six pounds
ten shillings per month.   Needless to say, I did not remain long
there.

The chief officer's wages were twelve pounds per month—a man
over forty years of age, who had been over twenty years at sea.   A
great number of officers in those liners had been in command in
sail before they joined as junior officers, and became so disgusted
that they threw the jobs up and went back to sail.   Good discipline
was maintained on board those liners, and an officer's word was
law.   Men of a turbulent disposition were logged and fined for
the least breach of discipline, and dismissed from the ship on
arrival at Glasgow.

Although these liner officers were overworked, underpaid, and
had bad accommodation, they were not so restive as the present-day
officers.   This is easily accounted for, as the officers of the period
had a very hard upbringing in sail, were hard worked, had bad
food, bad accommodation, and the usual hardships which were
experienced in every sailing vessel.   They did not know what an
easy life at sea meant.

The present-day officer is brought up under entirely different
conditions : he is paid wages while serving his apprenticeship, he
does not have to go aloft to furl sails on a stormy night, he is well
housed and fed, and physically ought to be a better man through
having the good fortune to escape the privations and hardships
experienced under sail.

Sailing-ship apprentices had to pay a premium ranging from
£35 to £75, which was returned to them in yearly instalments in
lieu of wages.   Apprentices in sailing ships were terribly over-

worked on vessels trading to the west coast of South America. They had to work cargo all day from six o'clock in the morning until six o'clock in the evening, and about ten p.m. they had to be alongside the jetty with the boat to bring the captain on board, and very often had to wait until two o'clock in the morning before he turned up. One apprentice had to keep a lookout for him whilst the others lay down to have a sleep on the thwarts of the boat.

The apprentices in tramp steamers had a much better time, and had very little boat-work to do as the captains generally engaged a shore boat to take them to and from the ship. Apprentices' duties on board a steamer, however, are very uninteresting in comparison to a sailing ship. Chipping iron rust, washing paint, painting and sweeping holds, become very monotonous.

Printed by W. R. MACKINTOSH, *The Orcadian* Office,
Victoria Street, Kirkwall.